# TEENAGE DIRTBAGS
## A BRIEF HISTORY OF THE MTV2 GENERATION
### (AND 50 ESSENTIAL ARTISTS WHO HELPED DEFINE IT)

# TEENAGE DIRTBAGS
## A BRIEF HISTORY OF THE MTV2 GENERATION
### (AND 50 ESSENTIAL ARTISTS WHO HELPED DEFINE IT)

### JON SHEASBY

TUCKER
DS
PRESS

*Teenage Dirtbags: A Brief History of the MTV2 Generation*
© 2026 Jon Sheasby

All Rights Reserved
Reproduction in whole or in part without the author's permission is strictly forbidden. All photos and/or copyrighted material appearing in this book remain the work of its owners.

Cover design by Jon Sheasby
Edited by David Bushman
Book designed by Scott Ryan

Published in the USA by Fayetteville Mafia/Tucker DS Press
Columbus, Ohio

Contact Information
Email: fayettevillemafiapress@gmail.com
Website: TuckerDSPress.com

*This book is dedicated to the artists featured throughout who have sadly passed away. Thank you for your music and for sharing it with us.*

# CONTENTS

Introduction..................................................................................1
1. MTV Killed the Radio Star...............................................4
2. Red Sky at Night, Rappers' Delight; Red Sky at Morning, Parents Take Warning!..................................................8
3. From Hanson to Manson: A Conversation with Grammy-Nominated Music Video Director and Graphic Designer P. R. Brown...................18
4. Antichrist Superstar, Are You as Evil as They Say You Are?..................36
5. Are You Ever Gonna Act Your Age? Well, Are Ya, Punk?..................46
6. Finding Your Voice Among the Noise: A Conversation with Actress/DJ/Singer and *American Pie* Alumna Lauren Mayhew..................55
7. Put the Pedal to the (Nu-)Metal!..................69
8. Smells (Kinda) Like Teen Spirit..................82
9. The Heavier the Music, the Nicer the People: A Conversation with Acclaimed Music Biographer and Magazine Editor Joel McIver..................90
10. New Beginnings, New Millennium, New Status Quo..................105
11. 50 Essential Artists Who Defined the MTV2 Generation..................110
12. Still Just a Teenage Dirtbag, Baby: A Conversation with Wheatus Founder Brendan B. Brown..................145
Bibliography..................161
Acknowledgments..................164
About the Author..................166

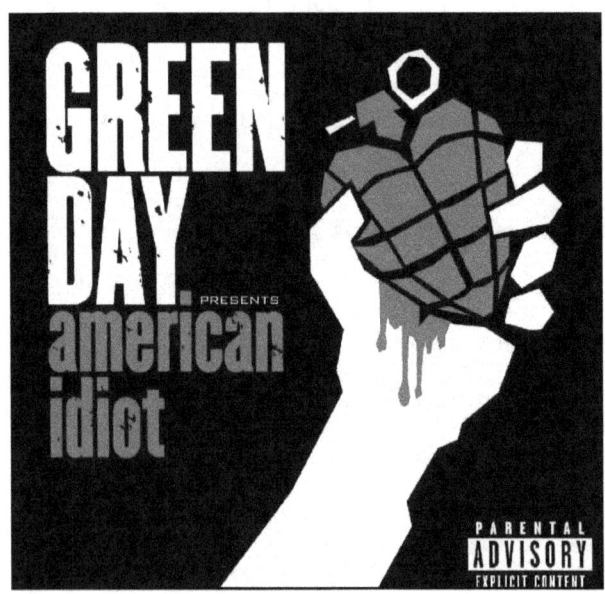

*American Idiot* by Green Day
Courtesy of Reprise Records

# Introduction

Before I was even in the planning stages of drafting this book, when all of this was nothing more than random notes on an otherwise blank document, it dawned on me that it had been twenty years since I had become a teenager. Two whole decades since the biggest struggle thirteen-year-old me had to deal with was choosing the right spot cream. Twenty years since possibly the most impactful record of my childhood, Green Day's 2004 seventh studio album, *American Idiot*, had been released. That last thought is the one that sparked what's written in front of you right now. I asked myself, "Can it be that long already?" I can't fathom how that time seems to have passed by so quickly, but in a world in which things shift so drastically day-to-day, I put on *American Idiot* and was taken aback.

It struck me how vitally important that album still sounds, even to someone from the UK, with its themes of societal breakdown and its condemnation of the Iraq War. The antiwar anthem "Holiday" made me think of Pink Floyd and Andriy Khlyvnyuk's 2022 song "Hey, Hey, Rise Up!," recorded in protest of Russia's invasion of Ukraine. It made me realize, when comparing Green Day's dismantlement of President George W. Bush on the album's title track, "American Idiot," to Eminem's savage 2017 anti-Trump freestyle, "The Storm," how little the world's changed. And although Green Day's lyrics didn't result in a visit from the Secret Service, something Eminem had the displeasure of experiencing because of his anti-Trump stance, the band's music still holds weight two decades on.

It's genuinely quite a trip to read the lyrics to "American Idiot" and imagine a scenario in which Green Day had some foresight into Donald

Trump, then of *The Apprentice* fame, coming to power and manipulating the term "fake news" throughout his time in office, misusing it as a way to preserve his fragile ego by controlling the narrative of negative press he wanted to bury. It's also as if Green Day had some insight into the future virtual information world of social networking. In particular, Elon Musk's $44 billion purchase of Twitter and his seemingly endless quest to spread propaganda, conspiracies, and disinformation at any personal or monetary cost. (Starting in 2019, Green Day would change the lyrics to "American Idiot" by referring to Trump's "MAGA agenda.")

*American Idiot* is both a timeless classic and a timely reminder that the more things change, the more they stay the same. A sad comment on today's politically tumultuous climate, indeed, but it signifies the importance of music and artistic expression, even within the supposed limitations of pop-punk, giving a voice to the average suburban teen awkwardly navigating their way through an alien world. However, it was ten years before Green Day was voicing its disillusion with the state of the world on *American Idiot* that the band first shot to fame with its seminal 1994 double-diamond-certified third studio album, *Dookie*, which shattered the glass ceiling for both existing and future agitators, like the Offspring and Avril Lavigne, respectively. But that's only one small part of the story . . .

Sandwiched between *Dookie* and *American Idiot* is *Enema of the State*, the 1999 third studio album by Blink-182, a band which was all too happy to be the MTV2 Generation's comic relief, expressing its emotional maturity—or lack thereof—with songs like "What's My Age Again?" These two bands, among hundreds of artists from the era, were crucial to my musical taste's development, and one specific channel, MTV2, was the place to see all these acts on rotation. Be it the infantile journals of Blink-182 or the political statements of Green Day, the mid-to-late 1990s and the 2000s were a great time to start one's popular music education. And with music channels quickly becoming a thing of the past, I'll treasure the prestreaming memories of channel surfing before they all disappear.

Including some of the most recognizable bands, one-hit wonders, and notorious figures who defined a generation of angsty kids, what follows isn't so much a celebratory retrospective of the greatest artists of the era as an unvarnished account of a time in music oft maligned by critics and vilified by those too ignorant to know any better. Featuring exclusive interviews with those who were there, this book concentrates on a chain of events that took place across North America in 1999. Events that followed the cultural phenomenon that was Britpop, Blur, Oasis, and all things Cool Britannia. Events that continue to shape the sound of alternative music to this day—making 1999, for me, the music industry's most important year over the past three decades.

From the rebranding of MTV2 and the major-label debut of the '00s best-selling-album artist to the music industry's implication in the Columbine High School massacre and the mainstream dominance of pop-punk, nu-metal, and post-grunge, 1999 saw a decade's worth of events crammed into a single year. At no other point in music history would you find a time when so many artists from so many backgrounds exploded into the cultural zeitgeist, allowing the freaks and geeks of the MTV2 Generation a chance to stand toe-to-toe with some of pop's biggest acts, selling millions of records in the process, and giving the alternative music scene a much needed boost after the decline of the grunge movement, prematurely set in motion by the 1994 suicide of Nirvana star Kurt Cobain.

But while there are plenty of reasons to celebrate the music of 1999, there remains a dark specter that looms over the year, full of heartbreak and tragedy, which unfortunately foreshadowed the challenging years ahead. Before we head back to the twentieth century's last hurrah, though, we have to take a short detour to where it all began.

So strap in, listen to the engine of the DeLorean roar, and let's journey back to 1981 and the birth of music television . . .

*CHAPTER 1*
# MTV Killed the Radio Star

When the clock struck midnight on Saturday, August 1, 1981, no one could have anticipated how the music industry would forever change over the next twenty-four hours. The birth of music television and the era of the music video had arrived. Kicking off with the Buggles' 1979 new wave classic, "Video Killed the Radio Star," MTV launched a global phenomenon that sent shockwaves through the music industry, redefining how an artist could visually present their music outside of the live setting. It gave emerging talents like Cyndi Lauper and Duran Duran a platform to express themselves away from late-night talk shows and magazine features. At the same time, seasoned performers like Genesis and the band's former singer Peter Gabriel reached a whole new demographic and level of fame.

The creation of MTV saw the music video evolve from little more than a promotional tool to a legitimate art form. Music videos for "Billie Jean," "Beat It," and "Thriller" helped Michael Jackson break away from his Motown youth and ascend to arguably the greatest pop superstardom the world has ever seen. Hollywood heavyweights like David Fincher, Gus Van Sant, and Antoine Fuqua would comparably find much success on MTV directing groundbreaking music videos before moving onto big-screen moviemaking. Furthermore, the 1984 conception of the MTV Video Music Awards (VMAs) sought to enhance the relationship between both mediums by honoring musicians and filmmakers alike, establishing a genuine rival to the music industry's most prestigious awards, the Grammys.

But even if the Video Music Awards and the MTV Movie Awards (launched in 1992 and renamed the MTV Movie & TV Awards in 2017) might not be as respected as the Oscars, Emmys, or Grammys, having the reputation of being the pop culture equivalent of a beauty pageant, it'd be dishonest to say they haven't been responsible for some of the most unforgettable showbiz moments from the last forty years. Who can forget Madonna's unfortunate wardrobe malfunction at the VMA's original ceremony in 1984 or Kanye West's infamous interruption during Taylor Swift's first-ever win in 2009? Besting both of those, however, has to be the iconic three-way kiss among Madonna, Britney Spears, and Christina Aguilera, which drew controversy and adulation aplenty back in 2003.

It's become easy to dismiss, especially in this digital age of social media influencers, how simple it seems to become an overnight TikTok sensation. But one cannot overestimate how life-changing it was to have your video played on MTV, with one specialized show becoming appointment viewing for older millennials in 1998. Before the days of smartphones, the decade-long original run of *Total Request Live* (*TRL*), hosted at its peak by Carson Daly, one of the most popular VJs in MTV history, changed the way artists interacted with their audience, giving them an up-close-and-personal look into their lives well before the creation of Instagram, and one can argue if the likes of NSYNC and Beyoncé would have risen as quickly and become as omnipresent as they did without a platform of its kind.

Admittedly, even if the MTV of the last twenty years (better known for prank shows like *Jackass* and *Punk'd* or reality shows like *The Osbournes* and *Jersey Shore*) bears little resemblance to the one of yesteryear, the channel's influence on the world of music—and television in general—is undeniable. Its success established a path for many sister channels and worldwide affiliates, granting a dedicated space for a diverse range of genres and up-and-coming musicians. In 1985, VH1 was designed to appeal to the adult contemporary music market by targeting viewers slightly older than the MTV Generation, and the 2002 launch of the urban contemporary-music-focused MTV Jams sought to capitalize on

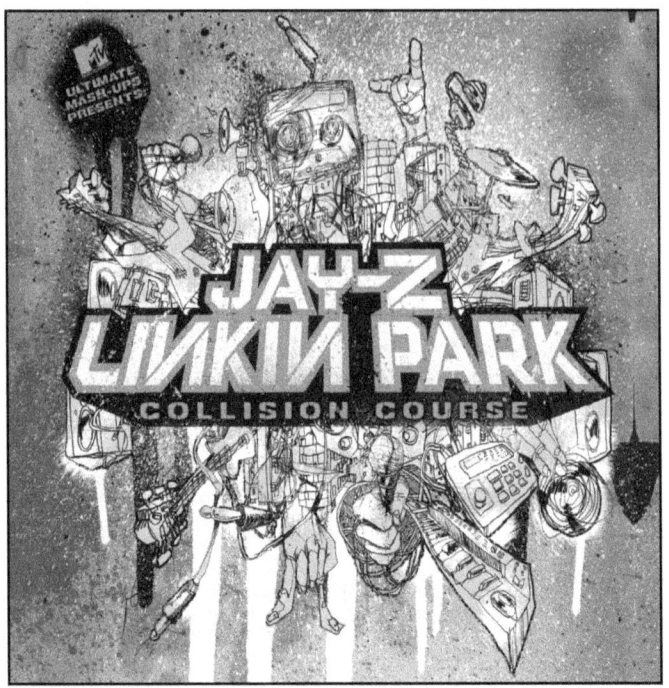

*Collision Course* by Jay-Z and Linkin Park
Courtesy of Roc-A-Fella Records, Machine Shop Records, Warner Bros.
Records Inc., and Def Jam Recordings

the commercial success of modern R&B.

In the interim between those two launches, M2, later renamed MTV2, debuted in 1996. If the MTV Generation refers to the teenagers and young adults of the 1980s and early-to-mid 1990s, MTV2 firmly targeted the adolescents of the mid-to-late 1990s and 2000s. It was MTV that brought international exposure to thousands of rising musicians in the '80s and '90s, but the 1999 relaunch of MTV2 put the spotlight on the alternative crowd, forgoing traditional pop music for the exploding pop-punk, nu-metal, and post-grunge scenes. A band like Disturbed, for instance, would achieve unprecedented success, with five consecutive albums debuting atop the US *Billboard* 200 chart, becoming only the third band to do so, after Metallica and Dave Matthews Band.

Linkin Park would likewise thrive in the new millennium, scoring six US chart-topping albums of its own. (*Hybrid Theory*, the band's colossal 2000 debut studio album, has since achieved twelve-times-platinum status in the US and has reportedly sold over thirty million units worldwide.) In an unexpected turn of events, the classic MTV show *Headbangers Ball* also found new life on MTV2 after its cancellation eight years prior. Its 2003 revival, hosted by Hatebreed's Jamey Jasta, became the go-to place to see the latest videos and interviews from the burgeoning melodic metalcore scene that ruled during the twenty-first century's first decade. Furthermore, crossover hip-hop artists like Eminem and Jay-Z would also see regular airplay on MTV2, strengthening the late '90s and early '00s affiliation between hip-hop and rock.

To illustrate this, the latter's 2004 collaborative EP with Linkin Park, *Collision Course*, became only the second extended play in history to top the US *Billboard* 200 chart, ten years after Alice in Chains's renowned 1994 release, *Jar of Flies*. MTV2's assortment of music would ultimately act as a guide for introducing a generation of people (like me) to music outside of the mainstream. As someone born in 1991, the music from my earliest memories consists of the inescapably formulaic sounds of boy band heartthrobs and teen pop idols. Manufactured groups like the Spice Girls and Boyzone were all but unavoidable, while the most left-field music to cross my path was the robotic sounds of Babylon Zoo's "Spaceman," which debuted atop the UK singles chart, selling over 383,000 copies in its first week back in 1996.

Pop music was in a healthy place, at least commercially, but the 1997 invention of AutoTune, popularized by Cher's 1998 dance-pop comeback, "Believe," caused a ripple effect in the industry, allowing less vocally talented performers a get-out-of-jail-free card when it came to being able to sing on key. But regardless of mainstream pop music's use of AutoTune and the almost ubiquitous use of such plug-ins in a business (supposedly) based on talent, little did I know back in January 1999 that just around the corner was an entire world of alternative music waiting to be discovered . . .

And, boy, was I in for a shock?!

*CHAPTER 2*
# Red Sky at Night, Rappers' Delight; Red Sky at Morning, Parents Take Warning!

Just one month after a new "Princess of Pop" had been crowned with the January 12, 1999, release of Britney Spears's debut studio album, . . . *Baby One More Time*, a polarizing challenger to hip-hop's throne would emerge from the underground Detroit battle rap scene with an alter ego intent on pissing off the world. With his comically violent doppelgänger, Slim Shady, by his side, Eminem experienced a rise that was nothing short of a fairy tale—a real-life rags-to-riches antihero with the heart of a poet and the mind of a serial killer. And whether he was channeling Leonard Cohen or John Wayne Gacy, it's Eminem who would help turn hip-hop into the juggernaut it is today, becoming Nielsen SoundScan's best-selling-album artist of the '00s with 32.2 million combined sales in the US alone.

But success wasn't always guaranteed for the one-time Academy Award winner, whose career didn't get off to the most auspicious of starts with his 1996 debut studio album, *Infinite*. Initially met with unfavorable comparisons to Nas's 1994 debut studio album, *Illmatic*, and distributed with little to no promotion by independent Detroit-based record label WEB Entertainment, owned and operated by frequent collaborators the Bass Brothers, *Infinite*'s release was limited to cassette and vinyl only, necessitating a hungry, twenty-four-year-old Eminem to sell copies out of his car. No actual sales figures exist for the record, which is believed to have sold no more than one thousand units, but its lack of success didn't deter the future megastar, who quickly went to work on his next release.

In 1997, Eminem released *Slim Shady EP*, his first and only solo extended play, giving him the chance to debut his new alter ego, the titular Slim Shady, and seeing him morph into the rapper we've now known for almost thirty years. Eminem's lyrics, inspired by the disappointment of *Infinite* and horrorcore artists like the Geto Boys and Three 6 Mafia, became more menacingly transgressive, juxtaposing his reflective Dr. Jekyll side—which spoke about childhood trauma, poverty, and addiction—with his recently developed Mr. Hyde-like persona, through which he demonstrated his cartoonishly problematic imagination and encyclopedic pop culture knowledge. And it's Eminem's ability to switch between personal admissions and controversial fantasies that caught the ears of two music industry giants.

Eminem's marked departure on *Slim Shady EP* displayed the evolution of an artist who was focused more on creating his own path and less on trying to appease the fans of his predecessors. Interscope Records cofounder and CEO until 2014, Jimmy Iovine, first recognized his potential after a company intern, Dean Geistlinger, was impressed by Eminem's performance at the 1997 Rap Olympics. Despite Eminem finishing in second place, a copy of *Slim Shady EP* was sent to Iovine, and so awestruck with what he heard, he contacted N.W.A legend and founder of Aftermath Entertainment Dr. Dre, who, similarly excited by Eminem's talent, tracked down the Detroit rapper and officially signed him to his record label on March 9, 1998.

This upturn in fortune couldn't have come at a better time for Eminem, against whom the deck had been stacked since the moment he was born. Abandoned by a deadbeat father and raised in poverty by a single mother, the child born Marshall Bruce Mathers III spent most of his youth bouncing around from state to state, rarely settling long enough to establish any roots, and was often the target of bullies in and out of school. Life for the then twenty-four-year-old Eminem wasn't much different, as he worked tirelessly—by cooking and cleaning at minimum wage for sixty hours a week—to support his newly born daughter, the frequently mentioned Hailie Jade, only to come back to an oft-burgled home in a crime-ridden neighborhood.

His arrival at Aftermath Entertainment came precisely one year after he was fired from his job at Gilbert's Lodge and evicted from his home, requiring him to move into his mother's mobile residence with Hailie and his then girlfriend—and later on-off wife—Kim Scott. After getting together with Dre, though, Eminem would fulfill his lifelong dream of becoming a legitimate recording artist. Released on February 23, 1999, *The Slim Shady LP*, Eminem's second studio album, debuted at number two on the US *Billboard* 200 with opening-week sales of 283,000 copies, a far cry from his two previous efforts' approximate totals. Not only had Eminem arrived on the big stage, but he was transformed from an underground rapper into an international celebrity almost overnight.

At the time of *The Slim Shady LP*'s release, seven-year-old me didn't even know what hip-hop was. I had no awareness of the infamous East Coast-West Coast rivalry that took the lives of both Notorious B.I.G.

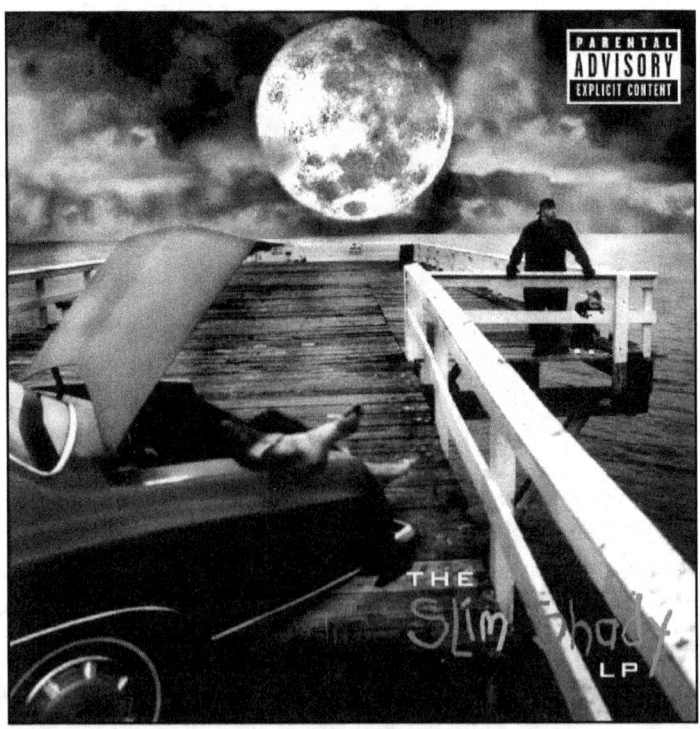

*The Slim Shady LP* by Eminem
Courtesy of Aftermath Entertainment, WEB Entertainment, and Interscope Records

and Tupac Shakur. Nor did growing up in the not-so-mean streets of Great Barr, Birmingham, really equal the street life experienced by those born and raised in Compton, California. To be honest, the edgiest rapper I'd ever heard up until that point was Will Smith, whose 1997 debut solo single, "Men in Black," the theme song to the blockbuster film of the same name, became the first cassette I bought with my own pocket money. (My sister got Aqua's "Barbie Girl" around the same time, which tells you everything you need to know about our early music tastes!)

I'm not saying we lived a sheltered childhood, locked in a cupboard under the stairs like Harry Potter, but our parents were somewhat overprotective. (Something only a selfish, self-absorbed teen could begrudge and something for which only an older, more world-weary person can be grateful.) You see, my parents were born in the 1950s. They grew up listening to the bands from the British Invasion, Motown, and all those emerging from Laurel Canyon. There were no Run-D.M.C. records lying around the house, nor would you hear Outkast playing through the car stereo. Hip-hop was just not on their radar. By the time my sister and I were born, though, music from the 1990s' golden age of hip-hop saw the genre fully transition into one of the music industry's most marketable exports.

And benefiting from the likes of A Tribe Called Quest and Snoop Dogg's success was Eminem, who became the first music artist I, as a kid, felt was speaking directly to me. I can distinctly remember seeing the music video for "My Name Is," *The Slim Shady LP*'s first single, for the first time and wondering what on earth I had stumbled upon. I had never seen—or heard—anything like it! The video for "My Name Is," which premiered on *TRL* in the US on January 21, 1999, gave me my first glimpse of the otherworldly androgynous Marilyn Manson (as impersonated by Eminem), saw him mimic everyone from President Bill Clinton to Johnny Carson, and contains a reference to Nine Inch Nails (the first time I'd ever heard those three words used in that sequential order).

I was enraptured by his lyrical wordplay, in which he cites the Spice Girls, the Incredible Hulk, and Pamela Anderson. And, to this day, I'm still astonished at how Eminem bends words to connect tongue-twisting rhymes to head-bopping melodies. I knew I was seeing—and hearing—something different, but I wasn't then old enough to be able to articulate why. I can say, however, that the video for "My Name Is" started a lifelong enthusiasm for an artist I can confidently say changed everything I knew about music. I was captivated from the start, and Eminem inspired me to appreciate songwriting from a new perspective. No longer was music just a passive diversion. It had become something more—an intellectually stimulating subject. This is why Eminem is—and shall remain—my favorite ever artist.

In my opinion, Eminem as a storyteller is arguably rivaled only by two of his fellow American raconteurs, Bob Dylan and Bruce Springsteen, both of whom have spent their lives standing up for the working class with their poignant and socially conscious lyrics. Dylan, in fact, has gone on record as recently as 2022, in an interview conducted by *The Wall Street Journal*, with his admiration for Eminem and fellow hip-hop trailblazer Wu-Tang Clan by saying he enjoys those "with a feeling for words and language" and "anybody whose vision parallels mine." And it's to the credit of these artists that we, the average citizens of the world, can still relate to Dylan, Springsteen, and Eminem and find unity in their words despite their combined net worth amounting to more than the annual GDP of a small island nation.

No generation gets lucky enough to escape the sins of its ancestors, and often we look to outside sources—like music, film, books, etc.—to better understand the human condition. A song like "Mosh," for instance, an anti-George W. Bush track criticizing America's actions during the "war on terror," on Eminem's 2004 fifth studio album, *Encore*, is every bit as politically charged as Dylan's "Blowin' in the Wind" or Springsteen's "Born in the U.S.A.," and it's these kinds of protest songs that remain as universally relevant today as on the day they were recorded. To be sure, it's somewhat of a conundrum for wealthy artists to continue to speak about the common person when fame and fortune have given their families financial security for generations to come, but to whom else are we supposed to aspire?

Tech bros who could end world hunger with a single bank transaction but are otherwise too concerned with morally corrupt election tampering? World leaders and politicians who are too invested in profiting from war instead of solving their own country's problems? I don't think so. On the visual side of things, Eminem separated himself from the posturing, hypermasculine, gangsta rap bravado of the '00s with his lampoonery, often dressing as an exaggerated version of celebrities and famous characters from pop culture in what must be the most mortifying badge of honor in showbiz. (Though, all that time spent in hair and makeup hasn't been for nothing, as he's won fifteen MTV Video Music Awards from sixty-eight nominations as of writing.)

For example, can you even imagine any one of Eminem's contemporaries dressing up like schoolgirl Britney Spears from her " . . . Baby One More Time" video (as he did in his two-time MTV Video Music Award-winning music video for "The Real Slim Shady") or making a video like 2005's Best Rap Video-nominated "Just Lose It" in which he assumes the identities of—in order of appearance—Michael Jackson, Pee-wee Herman, MC Hammer, Billy Bob Thornton's character from *Bad Santa*, Madonna, and Blink-182? Somehow, I can't envision Eminem's peers—who were more interested in rapping about their acquisition of women, money, jewelry, cars, and any other materialistic possession worth its weight in gold—wearing Madonna's Jean Paul Gaultier-designed cone bra. Can you?

I can't tell you exactly why, as a child, I was so taken by Eminem's artistry, because our upbringing couldn't have been more different. Like ninety-nine percent of everyone I've ever known, I was lucky enough to be raised in a stable, working-class environment. I was not a product of divorce but, instead, raised by two loving parents. We were never ones to travel on extravagant holidays abroad, instead choosing to frequent our favorite staycations across the British Isles, but I never had to want for anything. There were always clean clothes on my back, new shoes on my feet, and hot food on the table, and I know how much of a privilege those basic necessities are when there are those parents out there struggling their way through the latest cost-of-living crisis. Honestly, I even enjoyed school and must be the only ginger-haired kid never to have been bullied. (Shocking, I know!)

How, then, I hear you ask, did I relate to someone over four thousand miles away who experienced a childhood so different from mine? To be completely honest, I think my initial fascination with Eminem was not because of his humanized struggles (issues that are far more relatable as you get older) but because of his more dangerous side: Slim Shady. This might be hyperbole on my part, but I can equate Eminem's contentious mainstream arrival only to the accusations that greeted the hip-thrusting motions of Elvis Presley, namely of being a menace to society, in a 1956 letter sent to J. Edgar Hoover, then director of the FBI. Ultimately, we know their art and artistry pose no real danger or threat, but it does set off alarm bells when you're exposed to it for the first time, right?

It's rather amusing to look back from this vantage point and see something so innocuous by today's standards cause so much outrage, but I do understand how more repressed generations (those who grew up before the internet all but destroyed the concept of censorship) could've been so shocked by something that was seen as—especially at the time—outrageously transgressive. I mean, it's not like in 1999 I could've instantly found a free hub of explicit adult content after tapping a few keys on my laptop. But Eminem was all over mainstream music television, rapping about stealing dead grandmas from morgues and throwing them on their grandkids' porches, as described in *The Slim Shady LP*'s knowingly antonymous second single, "Role Model."

Discovering Eminem when I did was one of those early moments of self-discovery that comes with identity formation in adolescence—things that become so deep-rooted in your psyche that they shape your future self just as much as the DNA inherited from birth. In the end, just a tiny taste of the forbidden fruit—like listening to an artist whose lyrics the *Los Angeles Times* said "are so clever that [Eminem] makes murder sound as if it's a funny act he may indulge in simply to pass the time"—didn't, in reality, pose any intrinsic risk or jeopardy to me. But that feeling you got from the act of doing something that would see your parents react with disapproval is what made the dopamine high of excitement feel so dangerous as a kid.

What's more, my admiration for Eminem as an imperfect, accountable human has only grown over the years, despite the public perception of his persona—a far cry from Marshall Mathers's private life—constantly coming under scrutiny for being violent and offensive (on account of his farcically nihilistic lyrics), whereas his use of (admittedly distasteful) homophobic slurs has even made him recontextualize how he uses such language. Gay icon Sir Elton John, Eminem's close friend and reported

AA sponsor, has always come to his defense regarding such matters, but that alone isn't enough to change the opinions of those who are offended by his lyrics—including his mother and ex-wife, who have sued the rapper for slander and defamation, respectively.

A $10 million lawsuit filed by his mom, brought about by lyrics from "My Name Is," in which he references her alleged drug habit (something she vehemently denied), cost Eminem $25,000—of which she received only $1,600 after legal fees were deducted from the two-year-long trial. (A second lawsuit, in which she alleged emotional damage from the first trial, was dismissed out of hand.) Eminem's lyrics to "Kim," the notorious first song recorded for his next record, 2000's career-defining *The Marshall Mathers LP*, were comparably met with disdain from his then wife, who sued him for defamation as a result of the song's graphic depiction of her imaginary murder, derived from his anger toward her during their first of two chaotically short marriages.

While these two examples might lead you to think there's more than meets the eye in the accusations of violent and offensive lyrics, Eminem is, by all accounts, a loving father and family man, having not only raised his biological daughter but also legally adopting and acting as the primary carer to both his former sister-in-law's daughter and his ex-wife's child from an affair. (This is in addition to helping raise his younger half-brother, Nathan.) So, I ask you, reader: We're all aware of separating the art from the artist to justify one's continued support of our favorite entertainers, right? Then we can also differentiate between creating exaggerated, slasher-film-like caricatures, as Eminem habitually does, to the crimes for which R. Kelly is currently serving a thirty-one-year prison sentence.

It's always struck me as odd that we can go out on a Friday night, head down to the nearest multiplex, and consume buckets of popcorn while watching Michael Myers's latest gory exploits in the never-ending *Halloween* saga, but there's still a discernible sense of taboo when that imagery transitions over to music. (One of 2024's funniest news stories came about after legendary death metalers Cannibal Corpse—a band famed for its extreme depictions of violence, songs like "I Cum Blood," and hilarious cameo in the 1994 Jim Carrey-starring *Ace Ventura: Pet Detective*—came under attack from Gen Z, who, thanks to the marvel that is social media, failed in an attempt to cancel the band after their introduction to Cannibal Corpse's ridiculously brutal lyrics and deliberately gruesome album covers.)

It's one thing to cosplay in a Jason Voorhees-esque hockey mask while wielding a Leatherface-inspired chainsaw, as Eminem often does while under the guise of his Slim Shady persona, but it's a different thing altogether to enact harm on the innocent around you. Even the late film critic Roger Ebert (who, in 1980, alongside cohost Gene Siskel, once spent an entire episode of *Sneak Previews* lambasting the original *Friday the 13th* and its slasher film contemporaries) would come to admire Eminem's artistry with his positive review of *8 Mile*, the Eminem-starring 2002 semi-autobiographical drama film directed by Curtis Hanson. ("Lose Yourself," the lead single from the film's soundtrack, would win Eminem the Academy Award for Best Original Song on March 23, 2003.)

In favorably comparing *8 Mile* to Albert Magnoli's 1984 Prince musical film vehicle, *Purple Rain*, Ebert suggests that from the outset, *8 Mile* "stands aside from routine debut films by pop stars. It stands aside from Britney Spears [2002's *Crossroads*] and the Spice Girls [1997's *Spice World*] and the other hit machines who have unwisely tried to transfer musical ability into acting careers." Ebert continued his assessment of *8 Mile* by saying that like *Purple Rain*, "it is the real thing" and that "Eminem survives the X-ray truth-telling of the movie camera, which is so good at spotting phonies. He is on the level. Here he plays, if not himself, a version of himself, and we understand why he has been accepted as a star." (Not bad for a first-time feature film lead, huh?)

Eminem is truly a one-of-a-kind artist, and I know how lucky I am to have been able to see him live (somewhat of a rarity given the small amount of overseas touring he has done during his career) when he headlined the V Festival at Weston Park, Staffordshire, on Saturday, August 20, 2011. The show was one of only a handful of European concerts over the last decade or so and was made all the more notable given he brought out his D12 bandmates, his Bad Meets Evil partner Royce da 5'9", and the one and only Rihanna at various points during the show. I honestly thought I'd never get to see Eminem live, so to see him headline my first festival experience will forever remain in my mind as one of the most memorable nights of my life.

I'll always be grateful to Eminem for being the catalyst for my discovery of the broader world of hip-hop, but I'm also under no illusion that part of his success—as a white rapper in a genre created and popularized by black artists—is because of the color of his skin. This is a topic he has acknowledged throughout his career, most notably in the songs "White America" and "Without Me" from his 2002 fourth studio album, *The Eminem Show*, the latter of which references how Elvis had also profited from black artists forty-five years prior. But as much as there's truth to both of those cases, it wouldn't have been possible for either artist to have achieved so much and remained so relevant without an appeal that goes far beyond race and class.

Whatever the case, all I know is I for one am glad to have been able to witness Eminem's rise as it happened—especially as he seems to have laid his Slim Shady alter ego to rest with the 2024 release of his twelfth studio album, *The Death of Slim Shady (Coup de Grâce)*.

*CHAPTER 3*

# From Hanson to Manson: A Conversation with Grammy-Nominated Music Video Director and Graphic Designer P. R. Brown

The design and artistry that goes into creating an album cover is every bit as important as the music housed behind its sleeve. More than merely a marketing tool, the visual imagery used to present a record can be just as transportive as the music itself. Can you even think about *The Dark Side of the Moon*, Pink Floyd's 1973 eighth studio album, without picturing the evocative image of a prism refracting white light into a spectrum, a direct nod to the band's legendary light shows? Or, in the case of the MTV2 Generation, how about the rubber-gloved figure of adult film star Janine Lindemulder dressed in a revealing nurses' uniform, the instantly iconic image used for Blink-182's 1999 third studio album, *Enema of the State*?

As one of the most acclaimed graphic designers, photographers, and music video directors of the past thirty years, Bau-da Design Lab founder P. R. Brown is as well-placed as anyone to talk about working behind the scenes of the music industry, having created era-defining artwork for Marilyn Manson, Foo Fighters, and Korn as well as directing music videos for Evanescence, Slipknot, and My Chemical Romance. I want to thank P. R. for spending some time talking to me about his career, and I hope you enjoy our conversation.

**Jon Sheasby:** Hi, P. R.

**P. R. Brown:** Hey, how are you?

**Jon Sheasby:** I'm good, you?

**P. R. Brown:** I'm doing well.

**Jon Sheasby:** I can't thank you enough for agreeing to speak to me today.

**P. R. Brown:** No problem. I'm just excited to help out.

**Jon Sheasby:** Great! Thank you. Well, my first question is, as someone who's spent most of their working career behind the scenes of the music industry—in graphic design, photography, and filmmaking—which of those disciplines first inspired you as a child?

**P. R. Brown:** Definitely graphic design. My father was in marketing, and I started working for him when I was very young, probably around eleven. I started doing kids' meals for a fast-food restaurant and found an addiction for graphic design. I went to college early for that and then worked in London for a while at Pentagram. Then I came back and worked with Peter Saville [Pentagram Partner between 1990 and 1992] over here in the US. Peter and Brett Wickens [Pentagram Associate Partner between 1990 and 1993] were both huge inspirations for the music side of things, so that led me down the music path with them.

**Jon Sheasby:** Do you think you were always destined to work in the visual arts?

**P. R. Brown:** I think so. My mother is a fine art painter. My father was in marketing. And I've been drawing since the day I was born. [Laughs.] I think I'm one hundred percent indoctrinated into the creative side of things.

**Jon Sheasby:** Was art something that interested you at school?

**P. R. Brown:** Absolutely, yeah. I left high school early and went to art school when I was sixteen. I knew that was the path I wanted to go down.

**Jon Sheasby:** Do you recall some of your favorite album covers from your youth?

**P. R. Brown:** Definitely the Pink Floyd covers. You really can't outdo just how powerful those were.

**Jon Sheasby:** I just saw [Pink Floyd drummer] Nick Mason's band, A Saucerful of Secrets, a few months ago. They typically play Pink Floyd tunes from the Syd Barrett era until *Obscured by Clouds*. It's a brilliant show.

**P. R. Brown:** Oh, fantastic.

**Jon Sheasby:** Whenever they get over to the US, you'll have to go and see them.

**P. R. Brown:** Ah, nice. I gotta check them out.

**Jon Sheasby:** I think I'm right in saying the first pop artwork you worked on—on which you're credited as a digital artist—is "Spooky" by New Order [the fourth and final single from the band's 1993 sixth studio album, *Republic*]. Is that correct?

**P. R. Brown:** Yes. My God, I forgot about that. That was way back in the day!

**Jon Sheasby:** What was the digital design space like back then?

**P. R. Brown:** It was a notch away from being an abacus. [Laughs.] It's the best way I can describe it. You're talking about the very early days of Photoshop. It was very rudimentary. You would try and do something and let it go for forty-five minutes, then come back and realize it didn't work. You had one undo, and you would do it again and see how you got there.

**Jon Sheasby:** I suppose it took hours to do things that would only take minutes today?

**P. R. Brown:** Oh, yeah. It's something your phone could do. It took hours. And the fact that we even called it digital art back then is sheer comedy. It's like calling someone an AI artist now. [Laughs.]

**Jon Sheasby:** [Laughs.] Did you work on "Spooky" in the US or the UK?

**P. R. Brown:** That was when I was in London.

**Jon Sheasby:** How was moving over here at such a young age?

**P. R. Brown:** I loved it. I grew up in Minnesota, which is about as American apple pie as you can get. And having never really left the US and moving over to the UK to go to the University of Brighton when I was seventeen—still Brighton Polytechnic at that point—was life-changing. Then I got a chance to go and work with Peter and Brett at Pentagram for a while, and I just fell in love with London. The culture completely changed my path forward from there.

**Jon Sheasby:** Did they scout you out, or did you approach them?

**P. R. Brown:** I did a cold call when I was in school. I went up and met with them and asked if they would take on an intern. And they did. I got very lucky. Then I ended up working with them at Frankfurt Balkind in Los Angeles when they moved to the US.

**Jon Sheasby:** Do you ever get back to the UK much?

**P. R. Brown:** I have been. I get over there and shoot every once in a while. I still have a ton of friends there from when I was in college. But I'm in Europe every summer and will most likely retire there. That part of the world makes a lot more sense to me than this part of the world. [Laughs.]

**Jon Sheasby:** [Laughs.] Just barely, though. The UK's not too great at the moment either.

**P. R. Brown:** Nowhere is.

**Jon Sheasby:** I'm not sure if you're aware, but today [October 8, 2024] is actually the twenty-eighth anniversary of [Marilyn Manson's second studio album] *Antichrist Superstar*'s release.

**P. R. Brown:** Is it really?

**Jon Sheasby:** Yeah! It came out on October 8, 1996.

**P. R. Brown:** Good God! That makes me feel old. [Laughs.]

**Jon Sheasby:** So how did your collaboration with Marilyn Manson come about in the first place? Who was introduced to who?

**P. R. Brown:** So that was a very crazy experience. I was really close with a photographer in New York, an incredibly talented woman named Jana León. Manson's team had approached her as one of the potential photographers to photograph Manson for the album, and while she was meeting with them, they asked her if she knew any graphic designers because they were trying to find a designer to design it. So she mentioned me, and then his management team hit me up and said, "Can you send over a portfolio?" I looked at my work at that point, and it was all Miles Davis and Blue Note Records covers. So over the weekend, I just created five fictitious album covers with crazy band names like Circumscribed. [Laughs.] I just created the most grotesque, violent-looking things I could possibly conjure. And ironically, one of the elements I created on one of those fake album covers was the symbol on the front of *Antichrist Superstar*. I think Manson saw it and fell in love with it, so I went down and met with him. He was at Trent Reznor's studio [Nothing Studios] in New Orleans. I went down there and met with Manson, and we hit it off, and then I ended up getting the design work. My friend Jana ended up not shooting it. Dean Karr shot it, who did it amazingly, and then I worked with Manson all the way through [the band's 2003 fifth studio album] *The Golden Age of Grotesque*.

**Jon Sheasby:** Was Manson already a notorious symbol when you started working with him?

**P. R. Brown:** No. When I first met him, he was the nicest guy on the planet. It was a persona with a clear delineation between the two. He's

*Antichrist Superstar* by Marilyn Manson
Courtesy of Nothing Records and Interscope Records

very smart, very book smart, and knew exactly the buttons he wanted to push. And then, through the process, his character and his person became one and the same.

**Jon Sheasby:** I think when you watch something like [Michael Moore's 2002 Academy Award-winning documentary film] *Bowling for Columbine*, you see the real him and how smart he is and how eloquent he was, and it's just a shame to have seen him fall down this path of, well, you know.

**P. R. Brown:** Yeah, it reached a point when the two collided, his two worlds collided, that I was done. I had reached my limit. And then things, as we've seen, have got progressively more destructive. It seems like he's trying to build a path back, and I hope he can, but he did some gnarly things along the way. I hope he turns it around.

**Jon Sheasby:** While we're on the subject, I have to ask you about the cover for [Marilyn Manson's 1998 third studio album] *Mechanical Animals*, which is rightly regarded as one of the greatest of all time. Can you talk about how that came to be and your thoughts on its legacy over twenty-five years later?

**P. R. Brown:** Much of that credit has to go to Joseph Cultice, who did a spectacular job photographing that and worked with Manson to develop the androgynous alien look. I came into that project after Joseph had already shot it, so I wasn't a part of it when they created the initial look. I went in and created the mythology of the design. I threw in a lot of the hidden messages that we put throughout that package that were deciphered by the actual jewel box itself. It's truly one of my favorite packages from a designer standpoint because there are just so many multiple layers involved in that. But it was pretty crazy to see that one blow up, and I think that was the first time I ever saw one of my covers in Times Square that was the size of a building. [Laughs.]

**Jon Sheasby:** Especially that cover as well!

**P. R. Brown:** Yeah, exactly. But I think a lot of that praise should go to Joseph Cultice for shooting a spectacular, fashion-driven, very David Bowie-inspired world. I think it was genius. Beautifully done.

**Jon Sheasby:** I think it's such a shame how that creativity has, sort of, gone away as we move more and more into this digital space of releasing albums only on Bandcamp or iTunes or whatnot instead of having that record in your hands and being able to appreciate it on a large scale.

**P. R. Brown:** I fully agree. Thankfully, there's been a resurgence in vinyl records coming back out, but I agree that it was truly an amazing time to go and live in a different world based on the cover. You could look at it, listen to the music, and get lost in that world. Whereas now, everybody's just lost. [Laughs.]

**Jon Sheasby:** [Laughs.] Yeah, a lot of album art today looks the same, or, as you said before, it's created by AI, and there's no variety in the visuals whatsoever.

**P. R. Brown:** The thinking changed. The thinking back then was how do you *express* the music through visuals, whereas now it's how do you *sell* it through visuals. It's two different beasts.

**Jon Sheasby:** Absolutely. I was also wondering if you ever saw Eminem's video for "My Name Is," in which he dresses up as Manson from the *Mechanical Animals* cover?

**P. R. Brown:** I did. I loved it! [Laughs.] As far as a character goes, I think Eminem's become a fascinating mirror of our society through everything he's done to kind of show us who we are.

**Jon Sheasby:** I couldn't agree more. I think he's just one of the best ever to do it.

**P. R. Brown:** He's just so incredibly unapologetic and owns it in such a great way. I've been impressed throughout his entire trajectory. He's extremely talented on a musical level, but then, on a conceptual level, he goes so much deeper beyond the cartoonish surface. When you dig deep, it's really pretty poignant.

**Jon Sheasby:** The chapter that follows this conversation is all about Manson and the US media implicating him in the Columbine High School massacre, and I wondered if you have any recollections from back then. Did he ever confide in you during those times, and what was it like for you, both personally and professionally, as you were working so closely with him?

**P. R. Brown:** Well, it was doubly strange for me because I was also working on Michael Moore's book covers at the time. So, it was bizarre when *Bowling for Columbine* came out because my worlds were colliding. But no, I don't think Manson and I ever really spoke about it. At the time, I thought it was ridiculous that he was being pegged for it, though from a marketing standpoint, it's precisely the world that was the best fit for him. He wanted to be the villain back then. It's tough for me to look back at it because, on one side, it was complete bullshit that he was pegged as the reason it happened, but, at the same time, I think he basked in it and took on the role of being the villain that people needed because they refused to let two children become the villains they were.

**Jon Sheasby:** So how did you transition from being a graphic designer to a music video director? Was that something you ever considered before the opportunity presented itself?

**P. R. Brown:** No, that was Dez Fafara from Coal Chamber's idea. I was doing the album packaging [Coal Chamber's 2002 third studio album, *Dark Days*] for those guys, and he basically said, "You need to do my video." I looked at him and said, "You know I've never done a music video in my life, right? I don't have any clue what it's about." [Laughs.] And he's like, "Oh, you'll be fine. You'll be fine." So I came up with the idea for "Fiend" [*Dark Days*'s only single], and the next thing I knew, I was on the Universal Studios backlot with seventy-five extras and a massive crew, and we were filming "Fiend" for Coal Chamber. I found a fascination and love for it and went full-on into directing afterwards. I think I've ended up doing around three hundred music videos at this point. I've lost count.

**Jon Sheasby:** When you look at the list online, it's quite a catalogue of artists too.

**P. R. Brown:** Yeah. A bizarre, bizarre range. There were times when I was working with Hanson and Manson in the same week. [Laughs.] So it'll probably be the title of my autobiography someday: *From Hanson to Manson*. [Laughs.]

**Jon Sheasby:** Perfect title! [Laughs.] I also think two of your earliest music videos, "My Last Serenade" by Killswitch Engage and "I Could Care Less" by DevilDriver, are among the most iconic in heavy metal from that time. And it's funny to think that both bands were just as fresh to the process as you, as both music videos acted as each band's debut shoot. Was there any trepidation on your part in your early days as a filmmaker regarding being on set as a director instead of at your desk as a graphic designer?

**P. R. Brown:** I loved it. It was a thrill. The funny backstory to "My Last Serenade" is that I was shooting another video in my studio the day before, and there was a set made out of three thousand rolls of gauze wrapped around PVC tubing. A light then blew, the gauze caught on fire, and it burned down the entire set inside my studio.

**Jon Sheasby:** Oh God!

**P. R. Brown:** And overnight, we cleaned it up, painted it, built the set for "My Last Serenade," and we shot it the next day in the same studio. It was crazy!

**Jon Sheasby:** It's lucky your studio was still standing.

**P. R. Brown:** Yeah, I'm very lucky. Extremely lucky.

**Jon Sheasby:** How long do those shoots usually take?

**P. R. Brown:** A music video, back then, was probably one day of filming. Twelve to fourteen hours. I think "Sing" for My Chemical Romance [the third single from the band's 2010 fourth studio album, *Danger Days: The True Lives of the Fabulous Killjoys*] was a couple of days, but for the most part, I would say ninety-nine percent of the music videos I've shot were done in one day.

**Jon Sheasby:** It's a pretty quick turnaround, then, from actually shooting it to releasing it to the public?

**P. R. Brown:** Oh yeah. It's usually done, cut, and edited a week and a half later.

**Jon Sheasby:** Are there any artists or bands you've worked with that particularly stand out among your favorites? I know you've repeatedly worked with Amy Lee and Evanescence.

**P. R. Brown:** I love Amy. I would do anything for Amy. Anytime, anywhere. She and the whole band are amazing. Evanescence is definitely very high up there. And she's just a good friend. I think she's a creative genius, and I would jump at the chance to do anything with those guys.

**Jon Sheasby:** I know you've also done a ton of work with Corey Taylor in both Slipknot and Stone Sour.

**P. R. Brown:** I love Clown [Slipknot percussionist Shawn Crahan] and Corey. Both are dear friends and another pair that I would do absolutely anything for. I had a blast working with those guys on the *All Hope Is Gone* [Slipknot's 2008 fourth studio album] cycle back in the day. And then, Corey, he and I have played over the years, whether it's book covers for him or some Stone Sour stuff and other things too. But Corey's a great guy. And Clown is just a creative madman, a true genius. It would be something if you could bottle an ounce of that man's creativity. He's impressive.

**Jon Sheasby:** You directed all four videos from Slipknot's *All Hope Is Gone* record, right?

**P. R. Brown:** Yeah, I did all the videos on that cycle. "Snuff" was my favorite Slipknot video, hands down, that we ever did. I codirected that one with Shawn [Crahan]. I love that.

**Jon Sheasby:** I think "Dead Memories" is a great one too.

**P. R. Brown:** "Dead Memories" is hilarious. That was shot in Des Moines, Iowa, or just outside of Des Moines. And I remember us trying to go to their film office to ask about getting a permit to shoot Corey walking through the streets of downtown Des Moines. They basically said, "Yeah, you don't need a permit. Just shoot wherever you want. If people see you're shooting and they get in your shot, well, that's on them." [Laughs.] So I tested it and had Corey walk outside, down the State Capitol's steps, in full mask as he walked down. Not a peep from anyone. No one stopped us. No one came up. It was amazing!

**Jon Sheasby:** [Laughs.] Just one of those places you can get away with it?

Corey Taylor in Slipknot's "Dead Memories" music video
Courtesy of Roadrunner Record

**P. R. Brown:** Exactly.

**Jon Sheasby:** Do you have any favorite album covers and music videos from your catalogue?

**P. R. Brown:** Definitely the Manson days and *Antichrist Superstar* for album covers. That was a fun one, and it put me on a different career trajectory from where I was. I was doing jazz albums before I did that, and I became the dark bastard child of the music industry for a while because of that. [Laughs.] And probably "Sing" by My Chemical Romance from my videos. That's definitely up there. It's not every day you get to create an epic *Star Wars*-inspired music video. That was a lot of fun to do. There are tons that I love, but that's the one I always come back to when people ask me that question.

**Jon Sheasby:** Yeah, My Chemical Romance were a huge band for me as a kid. And the band's videos, in particular, were some of the best from that era.

**P. R. Brown:** They're great guys. They're just super creative. Working with Prince [on both the "Crimson and Clover" and "Chocolate Box" music videos] was a lot of fun too. The first concert I ever saw was Prince on the Purple Rain Tour, so working with him was a big moment for me. It was the only time I've ever had a set completely stop what they were doing to watch the artist. You could hear a pin drop on that set.

**Jon Sheasby:** I can imagine, yeah. Unbelievable.

**P. R. Brown:** It was. It was a great day.

**Jon Sheasby:** Did he still have that aura about him?

**P. R. Brown:** Oh yeah, absolutely. He walked in, and it was like a god coming on the set. He was very nice, but it was just like the world stopped.

**Jon Sheasby:** Getting to direct the music video for a Bond theme [Jack White and Alicia Keys's 2008 duet, "Another Way to Die," from *Quantum of Solace*] must've been a cool experience too, right? Especially as you got a nomination [for Best Short Form Music Video] at the 2009 Grammy Awards.

**P. R. Brown:** That was a lot of fun. And I ended up in Europe—in Paris, France—doing all the postproduction for two weeks. I loved it. They were both great. It was a lot of fun to go and create in that world, and being a part of the Bond experience was a blast.

**Jon Sheasby:** Was that something you were offered or had to pitch on?

**P. R. Brown:** It was like any music video back then—it was me pitching against fifteen to twenty other directors. That was always how it went down, for the most part, unless it was people with whom I had a very close relationship. But most of the time, it was writing pitches against multiple directors.

**Jon Sheasby:** Does that get to be a bit of a pain in the ass?

**P. R. Brown:** It does. I think there's a book somewhere full of hundreds and hundreds of treatment ideas that were never made.

**Jon Sheasby:** You got a Grammy nomination out of it, though, so it must have been worth it in the end, no?

**P. R. Brown:** Oh, it was good. It was fun. And I got to take my dad to the Grammys. It was a good day.

**Jon Sheasby:** Does that sort of success open the doors to the world of commercial filmmaking with the likes of Ford and PepsiCo?

**P. R. Brown:** I don't know if it opens the doors as much as it gives you the tools to break down those doors; I think that would be a better way to say it. [Laughs.] That's what music videos did for me. It was literally a boot camp on all kinds of filming and creative thinking that led to trying to make a dent in the commercial world, which is even more competitive than the music video world.

**Jon Sheasby:** How do the two compare?

**P. R. Brown:** I think there's a lot more artistic serenity in music videos, at least from the music videos that I like to do, versus commercials, where you're very much selling a product to your viewer or creating a specific message to go to a specific group of people informed by a committee. It's a very different process between both. That doesn't mean you can't be creative in commercials—it's just not on the same level. I equated it more to being a fine art photographer versus a studio portrait photographer. They're very different. Each has its own value, but the approaches differ.

**Jon Sheasby:** And out of all your ventures—in graphic design, photography, and filmmaking—which remains your biggest passion?

**P. R. Brown:** Photography. If and when I ever retire, I will live in some small town in the south of France and shoot fine art photography for the rest of my life, and I'd be quite happy.

**Jon Sheasby:** Is that something you love doing in your downtime?

**P. R. Brown:** All the time. My camera's always with me. When I travel, my vacations are planned around where I can shoot, much to my wife's chagrin. [Laughs.] There's a beauty—for me, at least—in fine art photography. I'm not answering to anyone. Even when I did all my work for the music industry, I was still selling a band's product. With fine art photography, I can be and just create for the sake of creating without any real intent on doing anything with it other than just enjoying the process and the experience of doing it. So, that's why I have such a great love for it.

**Jon Sheasby:** Do you ever think you'll release a book containing all your photography?

**P. R. Brown:** I think so at some point. We were laughing before about the diversity of my work and some of the music acts with whom I've worked, and that same diversity has followed me on any creative endeavor I've done. So when it comes to making a fine art book, how do I do it? Is it model based? Is it landscapes? Is it odd macros? That same diversity in my photography has always existed in my design and filmmaking, so it's hard for me to pull together a comprehensive book unless it's based on one subject, which I could do, but that's probably the thing holding me back. How do you create a version of a photobook that goes all over the place and get an audience to understand it?

**Jon Sheasby:** Totally. Have you ever been approached about doing a book?

**P. R. Brown:** I've had talks here and there, but it's never gone anywhere serious. It's just more in the back of my head that I know, at some point, I'll want to do it. I've shot live bands forever too, and I could easily do a few books on that. That may be a segue into it. Just to get through the experience and then, ultimately, do it for the sake of art after.

**Jon Sheasby:** What about film and TV?

**P. R. Brown:** I've definitely been attached to a few films throughout my career. And they were greenlit, but they all fell apart. And, over time, I just lost interest. It's such a cutthroat industry that I feel like I would have to sell so much of my soul to do it that it just never became worth it. Corey from Slipknot and I almost did a TV show that we can hopefully resurrect at some point. That's something I would definitely go back to. It was just a really cool idea.

**Jon Sheasby:** I know Corey's been getting into acting in the past few years, and that seems like a path he wants to explore more.

**P. R. Brown:** He's such a talented dude. He could do whatever he wanted. He's such a big presence, and his personality is so huge that it's a no-brainer for him to get into acting or any creative endeavor he wants.

**Jon Sheasby:** I think his writing is great as well, especially his first book [*Seven Deadly Sins: Settling the Argument Between Born Bad and Damaged Good*] and all the stories he tells from his childhood and how he can have a sense of humor about it. Things that would completely derail most people's lives.

**P. R. Brown:** I fully agree.

**Jon Sheasby:** How different is it, then, directing concert films?

**P. R. Brown:** They're fun. It's a totally different beast. It's me sitting at a control booth with seventeen different monitors telling seventeen different people what to do and what to shoot. It's a completely different experience.

**Jon Sheasby:** Are the takes extracted from a number of shows over a couple of nights or just the one?

**P. R. Brown:** For Evanescence [*Evanescence: Synthesis Live*], there were a couple of shows; for Mötley Crüe [*Crüe Fest*], there was one.

**Jon Sheasby:** How was working with Mötley?

**P. R. Brown:** They're great. I've worked with those guys forever, and Nikki [Sixx] is a really good friend. I always tell Nikki that I met him after he was sober, so it was a very different Nikki than his early days. The Nikki I met is an amazing human being who has been sober for the last twenty to thirty years, or however long it's been. And we just had a blast. Nikki and I would go off to shoot somewhere, whether it was Japan or you name it, and we would take a few days to photograph different areas because he's also a photographer. So we'd go to Bangkok, or we'd go to India, or we'd go to Cambodia and just shoot for the fun of it.

**Jon Sheasby:** It must be amazing to visit those places and be able to call it work, but it's not really a job when it's something you love doing, right?

**P. R. Brown:** Exactly. It's playing at its best. [Laughs.]

**Jon Sheasby:** So what's in the future for you?

**P. R. Brown:** Sometime down the road, I will get into some photography. Whether fine art shows, books, or whatever. That will be in the years to come. But it's been a glorious ride so far.

**Jon Sheasby:** Well, it's been a pleasure talking to you, P. R.

**P. R. Brown:** You bet. Thank you very much. Good luck with everything!

**Jon Sheasby:** Thanks. Have a good one!

*CHAPTER 4*
# Antichrist Superstar, Are You as Evil as They Say You Are?

Back in 1982, a TV documentary about *Les Prophéties* author Nostradamus, the alleged sixteenth-century prophet, inspired experimental pop icon Prince to write "1999," a song in which he imagines throwing a party before a disaster that would befall the world, as predicted by said oracle. However, with the countdown to the supposed Y2K bug and the potential catastrophic downfall of a world increasingly reliant on computers looming large, little did the "When Doves Cry" star know that the actual 1999 wasn't to be quite the celebratory party he had envisioned. But despite the fact the Y2K scare came and went, somewhat predictably, once the new millennium had begun, the music world was still reeling from its own crisis, inflamed by the (not in any way hypocritical) news media.

On April 20, 1999, the Columbine High School massacre ushered in one of the bleakest times in recent American history. The death toll of fifteen people, including both perpetrators, made it, at the time, the deadliest US high school shooting on record. The tragedy of Columbine remains one of the most infamous of its kind, and in its immediate aftermath, the press was quick to fire accusations against one of the 1990s' most provocative figures. Born Brian Hugh Warner, the enigmatic Marilyn Manson—lead singer of the band of the same name—ignited controversy from the get-go with his profane lyrics, outrageous live shows, and perverse artwork. Unfortunately for Manson, Columbine would be just the first of many times he'd be implicated in such heinous crimes.

Marilyn Manson was every conservative parent's worst nightmare, the 1990s equivalent of the counterculture iconoclasts—the Doors, Jimi Hendrix, MC5, etc.—of the 1960s. This time, though, the band's objective was not to bring about social change and equality for all. Instead, its mission was much more straightforward: to frighten the authorities and disturb the powers that be. And unsurprisingly, they did so with ease, evoking the frenzied Satanic panic incidents from the 1980s to such an extent that it became commonplace to hear the band's name and lyrics ushered throughout congressional hearings during the '90s and 2000s. Not only did Marilyn Manson succeed in its mission, but the band also comfortably ranks among the most noteworthy renegades of the MTV2 Generation.

With each band member requiring a stage name combining the first name of a pop culture icon (later members adopted a female sex symbol as their pseudonym) and the surname of a male serial killer (the *Portrait of an American Family*—the band's 1994 debut studio album—lineup consisting of singer Marilyn Manson, guitarist Daisy Berkowitz, bassist Gidget Gein, keyboardist Madonna Wayne Gacy, and drummer Sara Lee Lucas), from the outset it was clear for all to see that Marilyn Manson wasn't going to be the next wholesome, white-picket-fence, all-American band. This was not the second coming of David Cassidy of *The Partridge Family* fame. No, this was the unmade, alternative sequel to 1976's *The Omen*, in which little Damien Thorn grew up to live out his wildest rock and roll dreams.

Marilyn Manson was a John Waters movie come to life, a freak show of blasphemous anarchists hell-bent on infiltrating the mainstream. In 1996, the band ascended to the top of its class with the release of its second studio album, *Antichrist Superstar*, quickly gaining an army of die-hard fans, including America's favorite cherry-pie-eating filmmaker himself, David Lynch, who cast Manson in his 1997 surrealist neonoir film, *Lost Highway*. The band was featured on the film's soundtrack too, providing its 1995 cover of Screamin' Jay Hawkins's "I Put a Spell on

You" and an original composition, "Apple of Sodom," written specifically for *Lost Highway* at the request of Lynch, who was introduced to Manson by the soundtrack's producer, Nine Inch Nails mastermind Trent Reznor.

At the beginning of 1999, things were going well for the band. *Mechanical Animals*, Marilyn Manson's acclaimed glam-inspired third studio album, released on September 15, 1998, debuted atop the US *Billboard* 200 and was certified platinum less than six months later. Its success also earned Marilyn Manson the coveted headline slot, alongside Hole, at Australia and New Zealand's annual Big Day Out Festival, completing the band's metamorphosis into one of the premier rock acts in the world. But things would start to unravel shortly after when, on February 19, the band's lead singer filed a defamation countersuit against Craig Marks, the executive editor of *SPIN* magazine between 1991 and 1999, who had previously filed charges against Manson alleging harassment and assault, stemming from an incident backstage a few months prior.

Though Marks later dropped the lawsuit (and damages were settled out of court), 1999 wasn't about to get any better for the band's maestro. A thirty-seven-date North American coheadline tour with Hole, scheduled to take place between February 28 and April 27, was plagued by friction between the bands' respective leaders, both on and offstage and very much in front of the public's prying eyes, with only nine of the shows completed before Hole quit on March 14. Coincidentally, during the band's set on the final night, Manson himself suffered a hairline fracture to one of his ankles, causing the suspension—and eventual cancellation—of the once-promising Beautiful Monsters Tour. Then, as we know, Manson's life came to a standstill after the events of April 20.

In the years leading up to Columbine, Marilyn Manson had become accustomed to receiving scandalous negative press among the loudest virtue signalers (the band's enormous success supporting the notion that all publicity is good publicity) and, with the shock rockers swiftly becoming a key voice for the generation's disaffected youth, it was only a matter of time before conservative politicians (who repeatedly tried to ban the group from performing in various US states), religious missionaries (who picketed outside of almost every North American venue during the 1996-1997 Dead to the World Tour in support of *Antichrist Superstar*), and parental campaigners (who saw the band as a perverting influence on their susceptible children) made them public enemy number one.

Despite media speculation that the two killers were infatuated with Marilyn Manson, it was later proven that they had no interest in the band's music, nor were they inspired by the corrupting influence of which the group was accused. Michael Moore's must-see 2002 documentary film, *Bowling for Columbine*, which won the Academy Award for Best Documentary Feature Film on March 23, 2003, is arguably the definitive statement on the event and asks important questions as to how and why incidents like Columbine—and acts of gun violence in general—are so commonplace within the US. (The film also features thought-provoking insights from Manson, whose responses to Moore's questions are far

*Bowling for Columbine* movie poster
Courtesy of United Artists

more nuanced than you might think.)

Now, just to be clear, I'm not romanticizing Manson as some sort of saint, as he's been the subject of numerous lawsuits, pleaded no contest to a misdemeanor count of simple assault in 2023, and has faced several abuse allegations over the years. *Phoenix Rising*, Amy J. Berg's 2022 two-part documentary miniseries following actress and Manson's former girlfriend, Evan Rachel Wood, on her quest to extend the statute of limitations for domestic violence cases in California, paints a particularly alarming picture of toxic masculinity at its worst. But the news media's suggestion that Manson has any connection to the murders with which his name has been linked is an absurdly gross spreading of disinformation used to provoke moral outrage in an audience otherwise oblivious to the man's work.

If truth be told, in the simplest of deconstructions, the Manson persona we see in public is just one in a long line of shock rock malcontents who have challenged the norms imposed by society and opposed the censorship of art. Be it Alice Cooper, Gwar, Rammstein, or Rob Zombie, these acts use spectacle in a way that conjures the splatter-filled carnival atmosphere of France's legendary Grand Guignol theater, carrying on the tradition of pushing the boundaries of what's commonly acceptable to the public—expressly those who lean to the right—at large. But history has a strange way of repeating itself, and the attacks on Manson are no different to those faced by a whole host of performers who, in 1985, were met with the wrath of the PMRC (Parents Music Resource Center).

Cofounded by Tipper Gore, wife of career politician and environmentalist Al Gore, the PMRC's goal was to introduce a rating system to the US music industry, similar to those across the globe that classify films based on their suitability for moviegoers. The PMRC's agenda, dubbed the "Filthy Fifteen," focused on fifteen popular artists of the 1980s (AC/DC, Black Sabbath, Cyndi Lauper, Def Leppard, Judas Priest, Madonna, Mary Jane Girls, Mercyful Fate, Mötley Crüe, Prince, Sheena Easton, Twisted Sister, Vanity, Venom, and W.A.S.P.) and their purported objectionable lyrical content, arguing to restrict youngsters' access to this so-called explicit material through the introduction of a parental advisory sticker to be attached to any record deemed not to have met its arbitrary standards.

Just like the introduction of the Motion Picture Production Code (commonly known as the Hays Code) in the 1930s and the creation of the Comics Code Authority (CCA) in the 1950s, the regulations set by the PMRC were an attempt to suppress the vision of artists by those who otherwise had zero creative bones in their bodies. Unfortunately, on November 1, 1985, Gore and her cronies got their wish when the RIAA (Recording Industry Association of America) gave in to their demands to introduce the label—but only on specific releases of their choosing. This all went down while the Senate hearing into the "Filthy Fifteen" was still ongoing, but what Gore didn't expect is that while she had won the battle, she had very much lost the war of words with Twisted Sister star Dee Snider.

As one of the opposing witnesses, alongside eclectic rock visionary Frank Zappa and beloved folk singer-songwriter John Denver, to the PMRC's tyrannical proposition, Snider represented the world of hard rock and heavy metal with an eloquent rebuttal that rocked—excuse the pun—Mrs. Gore to her core, stating it was her dirty mind that found explicit meaning in otherwise inoffensive songs. The lyrics from one particular Twisted Sister track, "Under the Knife," taken from the band's 1982 debut studio album of the same name, came under scrutiny from the PMRC as it interpreted the song as being about sadomasochism and bondage. (In reality, Twisted Sister guitarist Eddie "Fingers" Ojeda's throat surgery inspired the song's lyrics.)

At the Senate hearing, Snider refuted the PMRC's position by saying, "Songs allow a person to put their own imagination, experiences, and dreams into the lyrics. People can interpret in many ways. Ms. Gore was looking for sadomasochism and bondage, and she found it." Ouch! Not only did the PMRC underestimate the intelligence of Snider, but the singer of the perennial MTV favorite "We're Not Gonna Take It" proved to the world that you should never judge a platinum-blonde, drag-wearing, spandex-suited metalhead by his appearance. The funny thing is that there's no evidence to suggest the warning label had any effect on record sales, and I know for a fact that a parental advisory sticker made me more intrigued to scout out albums I was told to avoid.

Mark Waters's 2002 comedy-drama television film, *Warning: Parental Advisory*, does a fine job of illustrating just how ludicrous this time was, and it's all the more noteworthy given the fact that it features an appearance by Dee Snider as himself reenacting the same speech he had made seventeen years prior. All this goes to show is that while the accusations made against Manson are far more serious than those experienced by the "Filthy Fifteen," it's familiar territory for subversive artists to be demonized by those too square to think outside of their self-imposed box. (This goes for other performers too, like Lynyrd Skynyrd, which was quick to agree with the news media's slandering of Manson, despite being all too happy to fly the Confederate flag for the better part of fifty years.)

Whether it's the Salem witch trials of the 1690s, the Satanic panic of the 1980s, or the shocking miscarriage of justice that transpired with the West Memphis Three in the 1990s, it's much easier to project outward and blame the wickedness of humanity on the work of the Devil instead of looking from within and accepting the evils of which we—as a species—are capable because of our own irrational fears and prejudice. It's one thing to oppose the actions of those whom you don't understand (I find the usage of Nazi symbolism by David Bowie, Roger Waters, and Marilyn Manson to be low-hanging fruit), but it's another thing entirely to suggest Manson had any implication in high school shootings, murdered Italian nuns, and Black Dahlia-inspired copycats.

Manson, to his credit, fought back in "Columbine: Whose Fault Is It?," an op-ed published by *Rolling Stone* on June 24, 1999, suggesting that deeper societal problems and America's gun culture, particularly the lack of nationwide gun control, were to blame. Manson warned readers that the hysteria generated by the news media's witch hunt was cause for concern, and it was the media that should shoulder the responsibility for the next shooting of its kind. "So is entertainment to blame?" Manson wrote. "I'd like media commentators to ask themselves, because their coverage of the event was some of the most gruesome entertainment any of us have seen. I think that the National Rifle Association is far too powerful to take on, so most people choose *Doom*, *The Basketball Diaries* or yours truly."

Manson, as an artist, will always have his detractors, and I'm not going to ridicule those who can't get on board with his particular brand of shock rock. After all, art is subjective, and it'd be boring if we all agreed to like the same things, because differing opinions make us all individuals rather than conformity-programmed robots. I will, however, always defend artistic expression and condemn those who try to defame the few who dare to push boundaries and challenge the establishment's power. "America loves to find an icon to hang its guilt on," Manson wrote. "But admittedly, I have assumed the role of Antichrist; I am the Nineties voice of individuality, and people tend to associate anyone who looks and behaves differently with illegal or immoral activity."

After a period away from the public spotlight and more than a year after the Columbine tragedy, Marilyn Manson responded with "Disposable Teens," the venomous first single from the band's fourth studio album, 2000's *Holy Wood (In the Shadow of the Valley of Death)*. Thematically, the record as a whole is a raging retort to Manson's scapegoating, commenting on the fallout from the band's implication in the tragic event and how society's unattainable idealism has failed the generation's teens. The album's subsequent two singles, "The Fight Song" and "The Nobodies," also explicitly refer to the massacre, rebuking the media's glorification of violence and the way it's exploited as entertainment, leading me to draw parallels to a whole stack of cult films that satirize that exact concept.

Films like 1976's *Network*, the biting Paddy Chayefsky-written/Sidney Lumet-directed satirical black comedy-drama, savagely critiques society's dissipating moral compass by seemingly predicting the vulgar artificiality of trash TV and the world's growing obsession with true crime's exploitative—and often nonconsensual—documenting of traumatic events. Similarly, both David Cronenberg's 1983 sci-fi body horror film, *Videodrome*, and John Carpenter's 1988 sci-fi action horror film, *They Live*, satirize the technological world of augmented reality in which we're brainwashed—or, in the case of *Videodrome*, given malignant brain tumors—by a malevolently capitalist dystopia that's become engrossed with political manipulation.

Although some of its not-so-subtle messaging may get lost in its feverish decadence, 1994's *Natural Born Killers*, Oliver Stone's ultraviolent spin on the lore of famed Depression-era outlaws Bonnie Parker and Clyde Barrow, is perhaps the most obvious comparison to Manson's argument. While disowned by Quentin Tarantino, the film's credited story writer, *Natural Born Killers* is an MTV-inspired maximalist commentary on mass media's glorification of serial killers, how they're treated as pseudo celebrities by the press (something that true crime documentaries are often accused of and are arguably complicit in), and how we—the consumers—binge on violence like junk food.

Like Manson, *Natural Born Killers* and its creators would get caught up in the storm that emerged after Columbine, with claims the film inspired several copycat crimes, committed mainly by fanatical high schoolers, including the two Columbine killers, who were proven to be fans of the film, having used the initials NBK in their coded messages. (As an aside, it's interesting to note that the film, like *Lost Highway*, features a soundtrack produced by Trent Reznor, plus a Marilyn Manson song, "Cyclops," taken from *Portrait of an American Family*.) But while the film's link to the killers is unfortunate, it's simply too easy to blame the savagery committed by sick individuals on violence in film, TV, and video games.

The vast majority of us know the difference between right, wrong, real, and fake. But, in my opinion, the ease with which real violence is circulated across the internet and social media—as well as exploited by the press—is far more concerning than what's found in fictional storytelling. It's sad, then, to realize that Manson, a man who once so eloquently said, "In my work I examine the America we live in, and I've always tried to show people that the devil we blame our atrocities on is really just each one of us," has lived long enough to mirror Harvey Dent's famous quote, "You either die a hero or you live long enough to see yourself become the villain," from Christopher Nolan's blockbuster sequel to *Batman Begins*, 2008's *The Dark Knight*.

But while I don't think it's in Manson's future to transition into America's favorite golf-playing pensioner (as has happened with Alice Cooper, one of the godfathers of shock rock, who, let's not forget, performed such increasingly bizarre stage shows in the early half of the 1970s that it led members of the British Parliament to encourage the banning of his namesake band from touring the UK), the self-proclaimed Antichrist Superstar continues to record and tour around the world, apparently unfazed by the accusations he has faced from both the press and from his former partner, Evan Rachel Wood, whose strength in publicly naming Manson as her alleged abuser will hopefully give other survivors the courage to confront their demons, too.

(On Tuesday, November 26, 2024, just four days after Marilyn Manson released its twelfth studio album, *One Assassination Under God—Chapter 1*, it was announced that Manson himself had abandoned his 2022 defamation lawsuit against Evan Rachel Wood and had agreed to pay her legal fees—a reported $327,000—in full. Michael J. Kump, an attorney for Wood, said in a statement released to the press, "[Manson] filed a lawsuit against Ms. Wood as a publicity stunt to try to undermine the credibility of his many accusers and revive his faltering career. But his attempt to silence and intimidate Ms. Wood failed." According to *Variety*, the agreement had been reached one week earlier, on November 19.)

## CHAPTER 5
# Are You Ever Gonna Act Your Age? Well, Are Ya, Punk?

At the same time Ricky Martin was "Livin' la Vida Loca" with the May 11, 1999, release of his self-titled debut English-language studio album (and fifth overall), pop-punk was quietly making its mainstream comeback after previously peaking in 1994 with the one-two punch of Green Day's *Dookie* and the Offspring's *Smash*. Jimmy Eat World was the first to attempt to break through with the February 23, 1999, release of its emo-tinged third studio album, *Clarity*—but it wouldn't be until years later that the record's brilliance would be justly appreciated en masse. New Found Glory's full-length debut, *Nothing Gold Can Stay*, released on May 1, 1999, also arrived to much acclaim but similarly struggled to make an impact in the shadows of Ricky Martin and the Backstreet Boys.

But as highly regarded and influential as both *Clarity* and *Nothing Gold Can Stay* have become over the past two decades, a California-based pop-punk trio was waiting in the wings to fully capitalize on the scene's dormant commercial potential and was mere weeks away from issuing its genre-defining third studio album. Released on June 1, 1999, *Enema of the State* instantly became the unofficial soundtrack for the freaks and geeks of the MTV2 Generation with its amalgamation of juvenile innuendos, massive hooks, and radio-friendly hits. The album's success likewise helped its architect, Blink-182, graduate from relative obscurity into a global rock powerhouse, turning toilet humor, UFO conspiracies, and hormonal suburban angst into timeless pop-punk anthems.

However, as with so many bands that came before, Blink-182's rise was not without complications that threatened to derail its potential before it fully surfaced. With Blink-182's first two studio albums, 1995's *Cheshire Cat* and 1997's *Dude Ranch*, only denting the worldwide charts (the latter peaked at sixty-seven on the US *Billboard* 200) and infighting threatening to thwart the band's future, drastic measures were taken to ensure that album number three would be its breakthrough. Gone was original drummer Scott Raynor, ousted by bassist/singer Mark Hoppus and guitarist/singer Tom DeLonge, and in came Travis Barker, whose infectious grooves revitalized the band, cementing their signature sound and completing the classic lineup we know and love.

By mixing the spirit and energy of 1970s punk with the band's signature trademark humor, *Enema of the State* would become the template for the future of pop-punk. Blink-182's music videos, particularly "All the Small Things," released as the album's second single and regarded as one of the band's key tracks, even mocked those made by the Backstreet Boys and Britney Spears, quickly endearing them to millions of fans and inspiring future parody videos from Bowling for Soup and Fall Out Boy. (In 2021, *Kerrang!* noted that the album contains "Twelve tracks of polished, ecstatic goofiness, undercut by moments of deceptively profound introspection" and that it "felt like the zeitgeist had truly been captured and pop-punk's floodgates had toppled.")

If I'm being honest with myself, my teenage dreams of being the next Slash were a bit of a stretch, but it was Mark Hoppus's simple—yet melodic—basslines that inspired me to pick up the instrument after trying—and failing—in my quest to become a six-string axe slinger. The guitar solo in "November Rain" may be far beyond my capabilities as a musician—or enthusiastic player of music, to be more precise—but I can honestly say I get just as much of an endorphin high out of noodling along to "Man Overboard" as I ever would from shredding until my fingers bled. And it's with those unpretentiously anthemic compositions that Blink-182 was able to replicate the success of its forefathers—the Ramones, the Descendents, etc.—who had changed the status quo of rock years before.

The first of four Blink-182 albums to have been produced by the late Jerry Finn, a man Mark Hoppus once dubbed the unofficial fourth member of the band, *Enema of the State* is just one of many records to have been blessed with his technical proficiency in helping to refine rough diamonds into polished gems. Be it Blink-182's *Enema of the State* or Sum 41's debut studio album, 2001's *All Killer No Filler*, Finn was to pop-punk as Nile Rodgers is to disco or Timbaland is to contemporary R&B. Finn's warm guitar tones and in-your-face sound mixes, fingerprints that can be found throughout the second wave of pop-punk, would also go on to inspire modern producers including Goldfinger lead singer/guitarist John Feldmann, who credits Finn's style as an influence on his own discography.

Feldmann, a self-proclaimed student of Finn's methodology, would—in a rather kismet turn of events—himself produce and cowrite 2016's *California* and 2019's *Nine*, Blink-182's two records with Alkaline Trio star Matt Skiba, who replaced original guitarist/singer Tom DeLonge between 2015 and 2022. In 2016, Feldmann revealed in an interview with *MusicRadar*, "Jerry Finn was one of my mentors. Whenever I could corner him at a party, I harassed him about how he gets guitar sounds and how he gets his mixes to sound so punchy. The guys in Blink didn't know that stuff happened, but they knew the sound of my records was influenced by the records Jerry made." (Besides producing Blink-182 and Sum 41, Finn worked with AFI, Rancid, and even Morrissey.)

While the band's lyrical repertoire has somewhat matured, thankfully, past scatological comedy and asinine tales of failing to get laid (breakups, miraculously surviving plane crashes, and cancer battles going some way to help its members come to terms with their mortality), it's irrefutable that a considerable part of Blink-182's early success was because of its uncanny ability to encapsulate the absurd dichotomy of the pubescent mind. You remember what it was like to be a teen, right? When everything felt like an explosive cocktail of hormones, existential crises, and peer pressure. The endless cycle of trying to act mature and wanting to be treated like an adult despite having little to no life experience and a brain that acted on impulse rather than reason.

Unfortunately, those out there without a sense of humor would like you to believe the entirety of Blink-182's discography can be distilled to nothing more than an ode to masturbation, dick jokes, and embarrassing teenage encounters with girls (as heard in "M+M's," "Degenerate," and "First Date," respectively). But that assumption couldn't be further from the truth. In actuality, Blink-182's evolution—dare I say maturation—to a more melancholic sound (as heard more frequently post-*Enema of the State* in songs like "Stay Together for the Kids," "I Miss You," and "Down") can be heard as early as 1997 in the now-classic track "Dammit," released as the second single—of four in total—from the band's previous record, *Dude Ranch*.

Blink-182's most significant leap toward a more profound tone, though, came with *Enema of the State*'s third and final single, "Adam's Song," which also got caught up in the aftermath of the Columbine High School massacre after Greg Barnes, a teenager who attended the school and was struggling to deal with the loss of a friend who died during the incident, sadly committed suicide while playing the song on repeat on May 4, 2000. As someone who knows all too well how the dark cloud of depression can be the most isolating experience imaginable, I understand how heartbreaking it is to know that the perpetrators of Columbine were not only responsible for the deaths of those on April 20, 1999, but also continued, after the fact, to take the lives of those impacted by their heinous acts.

But as much as "Adam's Song" examines the more serious themes of suicide and depression, at its core the song is about hope and finding the strength to overcome extended periods of crisis—topics that music handles better than any other art form. In 2009, Blink-182 retired "Adam's Song" from live performances after the death of the band's close friend and collaborator, DJ AM (Adam Goldstein), who passed away from a drug overdose on August 28, 2009, making Travis Barker the only surviving passenger from the six on board the South Carolina Learjet 60 plane crash on September 19, 2008. The band would later return to the song in 2018 and again in 2023 after Hoppus's battle with cancer.

Moreover, not only did the second wave of pop-punk go mainstream in 1999, but skate-punk also soared to previously unimaginable heights, owing a massive debt to the inconceivable popularity of *Tony Hawk's* video game series. The original entry, *Tony Hawk's Pro Skater*, which debuted just a few months after the release of *Enema of the State*, on September 29, 1999, is recognized as the catalyst for introducing skateboarding to a global audience, with its riveting gameplay and addictive soundtrack. Its competitor, *Dave Mirra Freestyle BMX*, which debuted just under a year later, on September 14, 2000, followed its footsteps, with both series' soundtracks—featuring Goldfinger, the Offspring, and Sum 41—enhancing pop-punk's mainstream reach.

But by far the most significant reason the second wave of pop-punk exploded in popularity during this time was the existence of the Warped Tour, the largest and longest-running traveling music festival in the US, which took place every year between 1995 and 2019. Traveling festivals were all the rage during the mid-1990s/early 2000s, and each summer, teens across North America—and later worldwide—were treated to assorted lineups comprising some of the most buzzworthy artists around. Following the success of the Warped Tour, new traveling festivals like Ozzfest (established 1996), the Family Values Tour (established 1998),

*Enema of the State* by Blink-182
Courtesy of MCA Records

and the Anger Management Tour (established 2000) would all come to fruition, signaling the commercial viability of such large-scale productions.

Later known as the Vans Warped Tour due to its sponsorship deal with the iconic skateboard shoe brand, the festival promoted an eclectic range of artists and genres, including skate-punk troublemaker NOFX, ska-punk luminary No Doubt, nu-metal pioneer Limp Bizkit, metalcore giant Killswitch Engage, and pop-punk mainstay Blink-182. While punk-adjacent artists would traditionally remain the festival's focus, it's because of this diverse field that so many artists broke big during the festival's run. Cherry-pick from 1999's lineup, for instance, and you could've found yourself watching the Black Eyed Peas, Blink-182, Eminem, Jimmy Eat World, Less Than Jake, and Simple Plan—all of whom would find noteworthy success in the coming years.

It should come as no surprise, then, that coinciding with this new class of pop-punk jokesters came a revival of the American teen sex comedy—the likes of which hadn't been seen since the mid-1980s. Featuring a cameo by Blink-182 and a soundtrack populated with pop-punk tunes, *American Pie*, Paul Weitz's 1999 directorial debut, sparked a resurgence of the wayward misadventures of horny high school teens during the 2000s and beyond. I must admit, I was far too young to appreciate *American Pie*'s metaphoric intricacies of sticking one's member into a warm apple pie, but I'll be damned if I don't give the film credit where it's due. (Weitz would later receive an Academy Award nomination—for Best Adapted Screenplay—for his work on 2002's *About a Boy*.)

Compared with 1981's *Porky's* and 1984's *Revenge of the Nerds*, just two of many problematic teen films that bask in their misogyny, *American Pie* has far more to say on the complicated minutia of teenage life, juxtaposing surface-level gross-out humor with a surprising amount of schmaltz. Take the absent parent or lack of adult supervision tropes, for example. Teens in '80s films were often portrayed as latchkey kids, a generation left to their own devices during their most formative years, potentially leading to any number of behavioral problems. In an indefensibly chauvinistic subplot, *Revenge of the Nerds* depicts rape by deception as a joke, actively wanting us—the audience—to root for the perpetrator, the film's theoretical protagonist, Lewis Skolnick (Robert

Carradine).

Thankfully, *American Pie* smartly rejects this archaic display of sexism thanks largely to the introduction of one of cinema's great dads, Noah Levenstein (Eugene Levy), whose positive guidance throughout the franchise—no matter how awkward and unintentionally embarrassing—would have benefited any teen in need of a sympathetic ear. Making *American Pie*'s favorite flute-playing band geek, Michelle Flaherty (Alyson Hannigan), the biggest nymphomaniac among the cast of misfits was also a stroke of genius, turning a longstanding genre cliche on its head by paralleling the "girl power" motto of the 1990s, a slogan originally coined by US punk band Bikini Kill. (In 2023, *ShortList* placed Noah Levenstein at number eight on its list of "The Best Movie and TV Dads of All Time.")

I don't think it's too much of a stretch to link glam metal's hedonistic prominence on MTV to the likes of *Porky's*'s and *Revenge of the Nerds*'s tactless debauchery, but by the time Penelope Spheeris's 1988 documentary film, *The Decline of Western Civilization Part II: The Metal Years*, had come out, glam metal's cracks were beginning to show, and it wouldn't be too much longer before its popularity was dwarfed by the introspective testimonies of grunge and alternative rock acts like Nirvana and R.E.M. These types of bands, known for their lyrical diaries of personal anguish, would open the world's eyes to a different kind of rock star, one (un)comfortable with sharing their mental health struggles and openly rejecting the decadent ideals that were commonplace the decade before.

I'm not going to pretend that *American Pie* is some grand late-twentieth-century feminist manifesto; it is, after all, responsible for helping popularize the word MILF in the public lexicon thanks to Jennifer Coolidge's performance as Stifler's Mom. There's also no question that *American Pie*'s target audience was the same demographic that made *Porky's* North America's sixth-highest-grossing film of 1982, earning an astonishing $105,492,483 (unadjusted for inflation). However, gone are the scenes that glamorize rape by deception, and in their place is a scene in which Noah catches his son, *American Pie*'s protagonist, Jim Levenstein (Jason Biggs), having sex with an apple pie, an act Owen Gleiberman, then of *Entertainment Weekly*, said had "shot past pseudo-exploitation and into the comedy of sexual role reversal."

In another unforgettable scene, *American Pie* cleverly subverts the traditionally fetishized male gaze—as conceived by British feminist film theorist Laura Mulvey—by reversing the typically masculine role of objectifying women as little more than commodities of sexual desire. Said scene, which features Jim and his friends perving over foreign exchange student Nadia (Shannon Elizabeth) via webcam, unexpectedly flips the script when Jim is then forced to perform a striptease for her pleasure. What Jim doesn't realize is that he's inadvertently shared the live-streamed footage from his bedroom with all of the internet (including an onlooking Blink-182), accidentally turning the voyeuristic gaze on himself, becoming the laughingstock of his school and, fittingly, the butt—quite literally—of the joke.

While there's an overreliance on unfortunate teen sex comedy traditions, namely gratuitous female nudity, at least *American Pie* made an effort to hold a mirror up to itself, reflecting back years of female objectification in a way that humiliates the culprits: the men. We squirm with embarrassment as we watch Noah walk in on Jim simulating sex with an apple pie left on the kitchen counter, and we're likewise mortified at the thought of being recorded while trying to perform a titillating striptease in front of our crush. (In 2019, *American Pie* screenwriter Adam Herz revealed to *The Ringer*'s Alan Siegel that he had vowed to make the film "less sexist than teen movies of the past" and that the film's characters "despite their misguided attempts to get laid, are, deep down, very sweet.")

There's also an argument to be made that the popularity of characters like Michelle Flaherty and Stifler's Mom helped open the door for more progressive female-centric gross-out comedies, such as 2011's *Bridesmaids* and 2017's equally raunchy *Girls Trip*, the first of which earned two Academy Award nominations, a Best Supporting Actress nod for Melissa McCarthy and a Best Original Screenplay nomination for cowriters Kristen Wiig and Annie Mumolo. In retrospect, I'm just glad to have grown up with the sage advice of Noah Levenstein, the autobiographical lyrics that make Blink-182's themes of alienation so relatable, and this new wave of female-fronted comedies that give the ladies a chance to prove they're just as crass as the boys.

In 2013, *Vice* published an article called "Can Pop Punk Age Gracefully?" in which its writer, Dan Ozzi, argues whether pop-punk is supposed to mature into adulthood. And on the surface, he has a point. The article singles out NOFX as one band that's not only refused to grow up but has "actually doubled down on their stupidity" through the years. Blink-182 wasn't fortunate enough to escape Ozzi's wrath either, as he ends his hypothesis by saying, "Every year a [pop-punk] band carries on is a year they grow farther from the material they wrote. Then, one day, they're standing on stage, and they look less like rock icons and more like dads chaperoning a high school dance." That's certainly one way of looking at it, I suppose, but it doesn't at all reflect my sentiment towards pop-punk.

Obviously, you'll never relate to songs about juvenile shenanigans more than when you were a kid, but people often misjudge nostalgia's effect on the transitional adult mind. We've all seen how nostalgia has nudged its way to the forefront of pop culture over the past decade, and while some would describe it as merely regressive sentimentality, what's often disregarded is how that wistful longing for a simpler time can be a powerful tool in regulating the erratic nature of one's mental health. Deep down, I don't really understand why people choose to be judgmental about what makes others happy. If you've aged past pop-punk, then that's totally fine. If, like me, however, you still love bands like Blink-182, then more power to you. Who wants to age gracefully, anyway?

If laughter is the best medicine, the MTV2 Generation had it in abundance. Every generation has grown up in uncertain times—be it war, economic crises, political unrest, etc.—and the MTV2 Generation was no different. I'm thankful, though, to have been exposed to the combined tomfoolery of the pop-punk jokesters of the late 1990s/early 2000s and the film exploits of the *American Pie* cast, whose farcical escapades gave an angst-ridden generation of kids something to laugh about among all the chaos.

*CHAPTER 6*
# Finding Your Voice Among the Noise: A Conversation with Actress/DJ/Singer and *American Pie* Alumna Lauren Mayhew

There were few things I loved more growing up than music, movies, and wrestling. But it's one thing to enjoy those interests from the comfort of your favorite chair. My next guest, Lauren Mayhew, has spent her career on the other side of the picture, having toured as a singer with Britney Spears and NSYNC, acted in movies such as *American Pie Presents: Band Camp*, and worked as a ring announcer for WWE (World Wrestling Entertainment). Lauren continues to break new ground in the world of DJing, and her perspective gave me firsthand insight into what it was like to be a young woman growing up in the entertainment industry during the late 1990s/early 2000s. I hope you appreciate reading this conversation as much as I did recording it.

**Jon Sheasby:** Going back to the beginning of your career, you began performing at an incredibly early age, appearing on the PBS children's educational musical show *The Reppies* and the long-running CBS soap opera *Guiding Light*. So I presume you knew you wanted to be a performer from as young as you can remember?

**Lauren Mayhew:** That's correct. I've basically wanted to sing, dance, and perform since I was little. I don't know if you know the actress Brittany Snow. She's a very successful American actress.

**Jon Sheasby:** I do, yeah! I loved her in Ti West's movie from a few years ago, *X*.

**Lauren Mayhew:** So I've known her since I was two. We grew up together, and our moms were very close friends when we were young. And one time, her mom asked my mom, "Hey, Brittany has this audition in Orlando. Do you guys wanna come? We can stop at the outlet malls on the way home and make it kind of, like, a fun mother-daughter double date." My mom asked if I wanted to go, and I obviously did. That was one of the first times I remember getting an opportunity to go and do a proper, professional audition, and it was such a fun atmosphere that I became hooked. [Laughs.]

**Jon Sheasby:** I understand your parents worked in the medical and healthcare industries, your father being an orthopedic surgeon and your mother being a nurse. Was there any expectation on their part that you would follow the same path, or did they support your creative side from the outset?

**Lauren Mayhew:** I think my parents pushed education more than medicine specifically. They just wanted me to do well in school. I don't think they needed me to go into the medical field, but school and education were really important to them. They said, "Just do well in school, and we'll help you facilitate making all of these things happen." And they did. When I was on *Guiding Light*, my mom traveled back and forth with me between New York and Florida. I think I was eleven or twelve, so I was definitely too young to travel alone and navigate all that. I was very fortunate that not only were my parents willing, but also in a situation where, since my dad was the boss, my mom was able to leave work when she needed to and take time off on a whim because I had an audition or because I was filming something. So it really was a dedication for my whole family and my sister because, since my mom traveled with me a lot, my sister was often with just my dad a lot of the time. I'm very grateful to all three of them, and I wouldn't be where I am right now if it wasn't for them.

**Jon Sheasby:** In 1998, you formed the girl group P.Y.T. [named after the Michael Jackson song of the same name] with three of your childhood friends, which led you to sign with Sony Music under its Epic Records banner, who released your first single, "Something More Beautiful," just a few months later in 1999. Did it surprise you how quickly things started to happen for the group?

**Lauren Mayhew:** It was absolutely bananas! It actually surprises me more now, knowing what's normal and what's not. I was twelve or thirteen years old at the time, and I don't think I realized how abnormal that was because, growing up in entertainment, as a kid I wasn't really paying attention to the business side. My mom was dealing with my agents, managers, contracts—all those things. It all seemed to flow together effortlessly, and I just had to show up and do the fun part. I was very shielded from all that stuff, and it was a similar situation when P.Y.T. happened. We weren't put together. Those girls [Ashley Niven, Lydia Bell, Tracy Williams] were my best friends growing up. We were in this group before, kind of like a live-performance version of *The Mickey Mouse Club*, except it was all girls ranging in age from about five years old to eighteen years old. The girls and I were in this group together, and we traveled all over Florida, performing at fairs, festivals, and corporate events.

They were just my best friends, and Lydia found this contest in a *Tiger Beat* magazine looking for the next big thing. So we decided to put P.Y.T. together and wanted to record a demo to send their way. We had gone to the director of the other group at the time and asked if she would help us record a song at one of the studios she used to create all the production for the group's performances. And she did, but before we even had a chance to submit the song to the magazine, she used her connections at Sony to schedule a meeting not even a week after we recorded the demo. At the time, we had done this TV pilot called *Divas*. The show was like *High School Musical* or *Glee* before they existed. She was just way before her time, and I was one of the pilot's leads. She had come to be connected to some people who worked at Sony to help pitch the pilot to become a TV show.

**Jon Sheasby:** But nothing came of it?

**Lauren Mayhew:** Right. Unfortunately, *Divas* didn't end up coming to fruition. But because she had made those connections, someone at Sony reached out to her in search of a new girl group. Sony was originally asking for girls who were sixteen, seventeen years old at the time, but she said, "You know what? Unfortunately, those girls aren't really working together. But I have these other girls who are much younger. They're only twelve or thirteen, but they're crazy talented." So she set up this meeting, and Sony flew down from New York to Orlando to meet us at the Peabody Hotel [since renamed the Hyatt Regency Orlando], about a ninety-minute drive from our homes in Tampa. We prepared some songs that we sang and danced to, and then we had to sing acapella individually and as a group. After that, David McPherson [of Sony subsidiary Epic Records], who would become our A&R, gave us the scariest talk I'd ever heard as a twelve-year-old girl.

**Jon Sheasby:** What'd he say?

**Lauren Mayhew:** Basically, how brutal and unforgiving the music industry was gonna be, and how we were gonna have to act like adults and work long hours and that it's just a cruel world. I remember thinking how intimidating that was, but there wasn't a piece of me that thought I couldn't do it. I think all four of us felt like that. The next day, they called to tell us we were signed, and we were like, "What?!" [Laughs.] At the time, we actually had a bunch of other offers because I was still on *Guiding Light*. I was also modeling for Wilhelmina, who was associated with Atlantic Records, and when they caught wind of Epic wanting to sign us, they also offered us a deal. Unfortunately, and this is a weird thing, when there are multiple girls and multiple parents involved, I think some of the parents felt that because the Atlantic offer came through my connections or relationships, they wanted to go through a neutral party, which I understand. I don't fault anyone for wanting to protect their kids. Looking back, we really should have just taken the best deal. I wasn't even really aware of any of this until much later when I had discussions about it with some of our management and my mom. So it's really wild how I didn't know any of this was happening then. I just wanted to sing and perform.

**Jon Sheasby:** Of course.

**Lauren Mayhew:** We ended up taking the deal with Sony and started recording immediately. We only had maybe two or three songs done, but we were opening for Britney Spears and NSYNC within a month.

**Jon Sheasby:** That's unbelievable!

**Lauren Mayhew:** Our labelmate at the time, Mandy Moore, was also performing and playing with us, and we just started touring immediately. You'll hear this theme throughout, but Sony was doing everything backwards. They had so much money to spend on promoting us, and they spent all this money for us to be out on tour, and we didn't even have a single that was ready and out in stores. At that time, they were giving away all these promotional CDs and stuff, but we didn't have a

Lauren Mayhew as Arianna in *American Pie Presents: Band Camp*
Courtesy of Universal Studios Home Entertainment

song on the radio. We didn't have a music video or an album. We had none of the things that we really needed. So, people saw and liked us, but how were they supposed to connect with us?

**Jon Sheasby:** Right.

**Lauren Mayhew:** We toured that whole summer with Britney and NSYNC, which is a lot of mouths to feed and a lot of salaries and hotels to pay for when you have a four-person group, plus two parents who are traveling with you, a tutor, a makeup artist, a tour manager, and a bus driver. That's a lot of people! And initially, they wanted to put us all in individual rooms. We were twelve-year-old children, so our parents put the kibosh on that. They were like, "No, our twelve-year-old daughters are not gonna be staying by themselves in a five-star hotel suite!" [Laughs.] To be real with you, as young girls, we wanted to be with each other. We wanted to hang out. It was like the best never-ending slumber party of all time.

**Jon Sheasby:** While P.Y.T. only lasted between 1998 and 2002, I think it's fair to say you got to experience more in those four years than most artists do in their entire lifetime. From touring with Britney Spears, 98 Degrees, and Destiny's Child to opening for Aerosmith and NSYNC during the 2001 Super Bowl XXXV pregame show, what are some of your favorite memories from that period?

**Lauren Mayhew:** The Super Bowl is up there, for sure. That was absolutely unbelievable! I remember, at the time they had given everyone disposable cameras, and I remember that when we started performing, they had lowered all the lights, which made all the flashes from the disposable cameras look like a million twinkling stars. It was just the coolest, most beautiful sight I've ever seen.

**Jon Sheasby:** You only got to record one studio album during your time with the group, 2001's *PYT (Down with Me)*, but how did that experience shape you as a performer and how was it personally encountering the ups and downs of the entertainment industry at such a young age?

**Lauren Mayhew:** So we actually recorded a lot more songs than what ended up on the album. We recorded some songs that were used for promotional material, and we also had a bunch of songs that were featured on soundtracks as well. But I would say one of the hardest things during that time, when you're a girl growing up, finding your voice both literally and figuratively, finding your onstage persona and presence and all these things, is discovering how people want to pigeonhole you into a particular area. I always had such a big personality growing up, and I was an excellent dancer. And even though I was a great singer and great at harmonizing and stuff, everyone always wants to pocket you instead of you being able to be good at multiple, different things. That was hard for me because it definitely did shape my identity and made me think that maybe I'm just not as good as someone like Ashley, who sang certain parts because she had this huge, belting voice, right?

**Jon Sheasby:** Right.

**Lauren Mayhew:** A lot of the time in the recording studio, I was brought in to figure out what the harmonies were and layer vocals and things like that. I wasn't given the chance to do a lot of the leads at the beginning, which was hard for me. It wasn't until later, towards the end, when we started recording other songs for soundtracks and stuff, that I came more into myself, into my voice, and realized that I have a good voice too. It just has a very different, more of a raspy grit to it. So, looking back, I can see that we were all good at different things, but it's hard to be around a bunch of adults when you're in your formative years and being told what you are or are not. Ultimately, you should be able to develop what you want to be and what you think you are and go towards that goal. And by the way, none of this is on the other girls. None of this is on them. This is about the adults and everyone around us, whom I also don't blame at the end of the day. It's show business, and I had to develop a thick skin growing up in the entertainment industry. It wasn't like I was necessarily bothered or upset by these things, but I wish I could tell my younger self not to question herself. I was just so nervous and scared at the beginning because of others' expectations of me.

**Jon Sheasby:** After P.Y.T. disbanded, you returned to acting, making your feature film debut alongside Hilary Duff in 2004's *Raise Your Voice* as well as regularly guesting on TV shows such as *Law & Order*, *CSI: Crime Scene Investigation*, *Dexter*, *9-1-1*, and *The Blacklist*. However, the role that sticks out for me is your turn as Arianna in 2005's *American Pie Presents: Band Camp*, a character who wouldn't look out of place beside the infamous Plastics clique from the previous year's *Mean Girls*. As *American Pie* is one of the definitive franchises of not only my childhood but the MTV2 Generation as a whole, do you remember what it felt like joining the series, and what are your thoughts on the film twenty years since its release?

**Lauren Mayhew:** I still feel incredibly grateful to have been a part of that franchise. I was barely a freshman in college when I was filming that movie—mostly in Malibu, California—so I was still kind of a tiny baby toddler. [Laughs.] And I remember I was going to school as a freshman at UCLA because, since I was a kid, it had been drilled into my head that education was so important. So of course I didn't take the semester off. No, that would've made too much sense! [Laughs.] I had a full freshman workload and was living in Westwood, Los Angeles, where UCLA is located, so that meant a forty-five-to-sixty-minute drive every morning to make my 6:00 a.m. call time. So I was shooting all day, studying for midterms in my trailer and juggling a full social calendar of being a freshman at a ginormous school. Once I almost fell asleep driving to set because it was still dark outside at that time in the morning. I remember calling my mom so that she could talk to me the rest of the way there. She actually came out on the next flight because I needed someone to drive me back and forth; I just couldn't do it all by myself. I later found out I could've had someone drive me, so then I was able to be carted around like a passenger princess, which was much more conducive. [Laughs.] But I loved all the people I worked with on that set, to be honest, and I'm still friends with many of them now. I've gotten to work with them later on, either as a DJ or doing other acting projects, so I've been able to keep in touch with most of them and watch their success, which is super cool.

**Jon Sheasby:** There are a lot of cool people in that film.

**Lauren Mayhew:** Yeah, absolutely. I remember too that the studio didn't expect it to turn out nearly as great as it did. It was made for the straight-to-DVD market, but they were so impressed that they almost took it to theaters, which I wish they had. Obviously, that would've been amazing for all of us. But, you know, it didn't end up happening. They had actually offered me a deal back then, a holding contract, to do the following movies in the series. But at the time, to their credit, I think my agents really believed in me, and they told me that they didn't want me to do another direct-to-DVD film and just be seen as the *American Pie* girl. I do think my agents were making the best choice at the time because there wasn't as much content being created and as many platforms/networks/streaming services as there are today—places where you can continually find new ways to reinvent yourself. Now, though, I wish I would've taken the deal because I feel like being involved in a franchise like that only helps one's career. There's not a straight career trajectory when you're an actor. There are ups and downs, and they are violent. But it was certainly a very cool experience to work on that film.

**Jon Sheasby:** Then, in 2009, you stepped into another arena, the world of wrestling and WWE, debuting as a ring announcer on the October 6, 2009, episode of *ECW*. How did your involvement with WWE come about?

**Lauren Mayhew:** That came about because after *American Pie*, I started auditioning for all this other stuff, and I was doing too much. I was trying to be a full-time student, taking summer school every year, and auditioning for these huge feature films and pilots where I'd have twenty-page scripts. Sometimes I'd have three auditions in a day, and I didn't know how to slow down. So, I think that maybe harmed the fact that I wasn't able to put my whole self into the roles I was going out for. I also believe that during that time, I went through all of these roles that were so incredibly dark, playing characters who'd been through a lot of traumatic stuff. And it was hard for me to relate to some of those characters who had seen a parent killed or had been abused because, back then, I didn't really have a wealth of knowledge or trauma to pull from to be able to really nail some of those parts. I had a pretty great childhood and lived a charmed life where my parents shielded me from many business aspects, so I think I was struggling with that. Then, by the time the WWE thing came around, I had graduated from UCLA, and I was pretty depressed, to be honest. Because, like, I had all these degrees that I didn't want to use and didn't care about, you know? So, what was even the point?

**Jon Sheasby:** I get that, yeah.

**Lauren Mayhew:** It felt like I'd lost my mojo and that I hadn't been riding the wave I had created for myself because I'd been focusing so much on my education. But I'm not putting down education. I'm still incredibly grateful to my parents for instilling that in me. I just wish I had known I didn't have to do it all at once. So when the WWE audition happened, I didn't really know, to be honest, much about wrestling. I think the last time I watched WWE was in fifth grade because a boy I had a crush on was in love with it. [Laughs.] I did the audition in Los Angeles, and then I got a call back from them saying they were gonna fly me out to their headquarters in Stamford, Connecticut, for an in-person screen test. It wasn't until I got there that I realized what a massive production it was, and I was just so wildly impressed. I was also just so glad to be back in a realm that was at such a professional level, so I ended up taking the opportunity when the offer came in. And I'm very thankful that I did that, but I don't think I was at all prepared for what that world was like. I'd done so many different things in entertainment since I was a kid, but nothing could have prepared me for what WWE was gonna be like. It's a whole other different beast of an animal. But I'm still very grateful, once again, that I did it because it was a cool experience, and now it's an even bigger brand across the globe.

**Jon Sheasby:** I was a massive fan of wrestling growing up, and when I started watching, WWE [then World Wrestling Federation] was right in the middle of its Attitude Era. During your time with the company, WWE transitioned to its PG Era to appeal to a younger generation and make wrestling more family friendly. While that decision has received much criticism from fans who grew up watching wrestling at its most violent, profane, and sexually explicit, the PG Era also laid the groundwork for the current crop of female talent in wrestling, in which athletic ability is just as coveted as sex appeal, bringing female roles in the business—specifically onscreen—closer to their male contemporaries more so than ever before. Was that shift in mentality felt backstage during your time with WWE?

**Lauren Mayhew:** I think they were, like in any realm of entertainment, trying to walk the line, which is the right play. I think it's important for females to be valued for their skill, talent, and athletic ability. But it's also imperative to be safe, and I don't think it's smart for women or men who aren't trained to be out there doing stunts and things like that without proper training.

**Jon Sheasby:** I fully agree.

**Lauren Mayhew:** I also think it's crucial to maintain the brand's integrity. But to me, it felt like the right move, especially as so many kids were there. It was interesting that they were never allowed to show any blood. The wrestlers weren't trying to make each other bleed, but even if it happened by accident, a cut or a nosebleed or something, I remember them immediately going to a commercial break. That must've been because of the restrictions of a TV-PG rating. It was funny because coming from the world of entertainment, the idea of being seen as beautiful or sexy was a lot more fashion forward. I remember I wore this one dress with all these feathers and stuff, and they were like, "No! Please just wear a more traditional, classic little black dress or something like that." That was really the only comment they ever made about my clothes. Yes, they wanted sexy, but they didn't care about the flashy stuff.

An issue I know they had before with all of the girls was that some wore heels and poked holes in the mats, which is obviously very expensive to keep replacing. So I remember they wanted all the girls to wear these chunky heels, which look terrible, with a short, mini cocktail dress. Super trashy looking. [Laughs.] I couldn't believe these things existed, but from then on, I never left home without these clear plastic stoppers with a cylindrical hole in the middle. You'd put them over the bottom of your heel, which would make it wider, but from a distance, it still looked like a skinny stiletto heel without the risk of puncturing the mats. So, I traveled everywhere with a few in case I lost some because I refused to wear a wedge. [Laughs.]

**Jon Sheasby:** While you continue to release music and act, including voicing Val Thundershock for seven seasons on DreamWorks's animated sitcom *Trolls: TrollsTopia*, in more recent years you've struck up a reputation as a renowned DJ, traveling all over the world and performing residencies across the globe. So when did your love for DJing start?

**Lauren Mayhew:** It came from me originally being a singer. I love writing music, and I've now licensed almost three hundred songs for use in feature films, national commercials, TV shows, etc. Everything from *The Voice* to *Dance Moms* to *The Real Housewives of New Jersey* and even the Emmys. I started collaborating with DJs and had the opportunity to go on tour with two DJs from Belgium, Thunderbuds [Thomas Hakkens and Phil Thijs]. This duo doesn't exist anymore, but I'd sing a couple of songs onstage with them every night, and I loved it. I was in bands and stuff, pop rock bands, when I was younger, but I always felt like I relied on someone to accompany me and complement my singing abilities. And, as a person who likes to be very self-sufficient, I wanted to learn about DJing. So at the time I was single and matched with this guy from Brazil on Bumble. I mean, like, you can't make this up. [Laughs.]

We had gone on this bike ride, and when we rode our bikes back to his place in Venice, California, he asked if I wanted to come in for some water because we were sweating our faces off. I went in and saw that he had all of this DJ equipment, and he asked if I wanted to learn. So I stayed an extra three or four hours and learnt some stuff from him. Then we were able to work around our individual schedules, and every week, he'd teach me literally everything from figuring out how to organize my music, how to operate Rekordbox, how to operate CDJs in a mixer, how to blend, beatmatching, etc. He ended up leaving California, but he was so patient with me, and he introduced me to someone, a guy called Peter, who continued to help me until I was ready to perform on my own. My first opportunities to perform were at underground raves and/or warehouse parties in Los Angeles, which Peter and some friends put on. I'm still so appreciative to have had those people help me; it was such a fantastic opportunity. I would always call him when I got my first massive show, the first time I performed for Tao Group Hospitality and played at Marquee and Lavo, or the first time I got my first residency or festival. I'd say, "Oh my gosh! You're not gonna believe this. Like, I'm doing it." And he'd reply, "I told you! I said you would."

**Jon Sheasby:** In terms of performing—out of acting, DJing, and singing—what would you say is currently your most creatively rewarding endeavor?

**Lauren Mayhew:** Well, I love DJing because I'm able to really create a vibe within the atmosphere of a crowd. It's also become a way that's allowed me to travel, see the world, and spread my music. But the most

DJ Lauren burning down the house
Courtesy of Lauren Mayhew

rewarding would still be singing, songwriting, and acting because I feel like I'm using more of myself—as an instrument—to connect more directly with an audience and fans. I feel like people can even more so get to know me and connect with me when I'm dancing and singing and able to touch their hands. Not that I'm not dancing my face off behind the DJ booth, but there's still an actual object in front of me—a physical separation from the crowd. With acting, what I love most about it is that I love being part of a bigger whole. There's something to be said about working with this massive team where everyone is incredible at their job and can see the final product we all made together, to make someone feel something, whether laughter or sadness or whatever, I think that's genuinely what film and music are about—a universal language that can cross diversity boundaries and language barriers and make people feel something. That makes me feel like I created something meaningful when I can do that.

**Jon Sheasby:** Well, I think that's a beautiful sentiment on which to end the conversation. Thank you so much for your time, Lauren.

**Lauren Mayhew:** No problem. It's been awesome talking to you.

**Jon Sheasby:** Likewise. I look forward to seeing whatever you have in store for us in the future!

**Lauren Mayhew:** Well, I'm always working on new music, and I'm looking forward to auditioning for more film/TV roles now that the [2023 SAG-AFTRA strike] is behind us. Plus, I've done a lot of voice acting recently, and I've just signed a deal to record a bunch of radio and commercial spots for United Parks & Resorts here in the US. So hopefully you'll be hearing from me very soon!

*CHAPTER 7*
# Put the Pedal to the (Nu-) Metal!

As much as I'd like to look back on the whole of the 1990s with a shiny pair of rose-tinted glasses, there's no getting around the fact that the decade became a breeding ground for misogyny in pop culture. Typically spurred on by the carnal (wet) dreams of heterosexual men, the '90s saw an influx of adult-oriented content that pandered to their most primitive desires. Tabloid scandals, for instance, became a public obsession, with paparazzi earning upward of six figures for a single snapshot of celebrities trying to evade their unwanted company. The internet was still in its infancy too, but that didn't stop private sex tapes—such as the one featuring Pamela Anderson and Tommy Lee—being stolen and circulated online without consent, a brazen violation of privacy.

On TV, the programming aired by the World Wrestling Federation (now WWE) between 1997 and 2002, a period in professional wrestling commonly known as the Attitude Era and widely regarded as popularizing the biggest boom in viewership in the sports entertainment's history, took the relatively wholesome theater of the spectacle and turned it on its head, promoting an upsurge in violence and sexuality to such a degree that the company's flagship show, *Raw*, regularly drew over five million weekly viewers in the US. Similarly, *The Jerry Springer Show*'s disputed authenticity only enhanced the show's ratings as it transitioned from a low-rated political talk show into a trash TV phenomenon, frequently pulling around eight million viewers per episode during its peak syndicated run.

On radio, Howard Stern—the famed shock jock host of *The Howard Stern Show* and star of cult comedy film *Private Parts*—became the most notorious name in US radio history after his remarks, including one particularly callous comment regarding the Columbine High School massacre, incurred around $2.5 million in fines between 1990 and 2004. (In 2004, Stern signed the first of several recurring five-year contracts—reportedly worth $500 million each—with Sirius Satellite Radio, thus avoiding terrestrial radio's obscenity rules.) Overlapping with these events was the 1999 explosion of alternative music's most polarizing subgenre, nu-metal, which to this day sparks just as much derision as celebration.

Most easily defined as combining the industrial heaviness of metal and the syncopated, record-scratching funkiness of hip-hop, nu-metal and its earliest adoptees—such as Korn, Sepultura, and Coal Chamber—shunned the speed and complexities that defined 1980s thrash metal by swapping traditional elements (like guitar solos and complicated arrangements) for simplified riffs and down-tuned grooves. The vocals heavily favored percussive growls over technical prowess, with rapping often—but not always—utilized as a bridge between hip-hop and metal. But nu-metal's roots can be traced back to the mid-to-late '80s, when bands like thrash metal's Anthrax and hip-hop's Public Enemy—both separate and in unison—began to merge the two genres to great success.

Before nu-metal became its own recognized subgenre in the mid-'90s, the late '80s saw the emergence of rap metal, an altogether more simplistic predecessor, which first found mainstream recognition when Anthrax—one of the "Big Four" of thrash metal, alongside Metallica, Megadeth, and Slayer—released the song "I'm the Man" from the band's 1987 EP of the same name. The song, which is both a parody of and tip of the hat to the style of rap rockers the Beastie Boys, features rapped vocals and samples from various sources, two common traits found throughout hip-hop. Also released in 1987 was Public Enemy's first studio album, *Yo! Bum Rush the Show*, which instantly struck a nerve among the musical elitists with its radical aggression and revolutionary innovative sound.

Public Enemy is known for its heavy use of samples, a production trademark of longtime collaborator the Bomb Squad, and its earliest tie to metal can be heard in "She Watch Channel Zero?!," the tenth track on the group's 1988 second studio album, *It Takes a Nation of Millions to Hold Us Back*. By sampling the half-time riff from "Angel of Death," the sonic assault that opens thrash metal band Slayer's landmark 1986 third studio album, *Reign in Blood*, fellow Def Jam labelmate Public Enemy unknowingly created an aural mashup that would inspire musicians for decades to come. Ultimately, the success of both Anthrax's dip into hip-hop and Public Enemy's experiment with metal led to their iconic 1991 collaboration, a newly recorded version of Public Enemy's 1987 song "Bring the Noise."

The original version of the song, on which Public Enemy's Chuck D namedrops Anthrax alongside hip-hop artists Eric B. and LL Cool J, thus acknowledging Anthrax guitarist Scott Ian's preference for wearing Public Enemy T-shirts onstage, started a mutual admiration between the two groups that not only resulted in the 1991 version of "Bring the Noise" but also saw them come together for a joint 1991-1992 world tour. Naturally, the climax of each show ended with Anthrax and Public Enemy performing "Bring the Noise" together, which didn't just help in bridging the gap between the metal crowd who came to see Anthrax and the hip-hop crowd who came to see Public Enemy but furthermore assisted in the future popularity of nu-metal.

The status of rap metal would continue to grow in the 1990s thanks to bands like Faith No More, Body Count, and Rage Against the Machine, the last mentioned of which scored two consecutive chart-toppers on the US *Billboard* 200 and has achieved platinum status with each of its four studio albums. The first commercially distributed appearance of nu-metal, however, came with the 1994 release of Korn's self-titled debut studio album. (In a 2014 article published by *Rolling Stone*, writer Christopher R. Weingarten marked the twentieth anniversary of *Korn* by saying it had an "unparalleled influence over the last two decades of American heavy music" and that the band "lurched into the world like hip-hop zombies rocking Adidas tracksuits, baggy jeans and untamed dreadlocks.")

*Korn*'s themes of bullying, drug addiction, and child abuse (as heard in the songs "Faget," "Helmet in the Bush," and "Daddy," respectively) established nu-metal's early tone as far darker than its rap metal precursor. The band's hip-hop-inspired clothing also gave the subgenre an identifiable dress code, which was later adopted by many of Korn's descendants. (*Korn* was also produced by Ross Robinson, whose name became synonymous with forging the sound of nu-metal.) In 1996, Brazilian metal icon Sepultura released its Ross Robinson-produced sixth studio album, *Roots*, which was not only heavily inspired by the sound of *Korn* but also featured contributions from Korn vocalist Jonathan Davis, Faith No More singer Mike Patton, and then House of Pain/future Limp Bizkit turntablist DJ Lethal.

With a style falling somewhere between the lyrical torment of Korn and the punishing grooves of Sepultura, Los Angeles-based Coal Chamber followed suit by combining elements of industrial, goth, and nu-metal with its self-titled 1997 debut studio album, directly inspiring a sound with which Slipknot would later find massive commercial success. But it wasn't until late 1997 that nu-metal's growth would expand exponentially with the arrival of Limp Bizkit, whose abrasive Ross Robinson-produced debut studio album, *Three Dollar Bill, Y'all*, abandoned the intensely personal lyrical style of Jonathan Davis and instead appealed to an audience whose misreading of texts like Chuck Palahniuk's 1996 debut novel, *Fight Club*, cultivated a community of pseudo masculine douchebags.

Exhibiting an altogether more hostile—some would say obnoxious—aesthetic compared with Korn, Limp Bizkit quickly defined the nu-metal style and attitude on which all future nu-metal bands based their act. The band's music combined chugging riffs with frantic bursts of energy, placing classic DJ techniques like scratching at the front of the mix. The band's lyrics were full of antagonizing rage and misanthropic externalizing and were, on more than a few occasions, denounced as being misogynistic. Limp Bizkit's bizarrely popular cover of George Michael's "Faith" even inspired one of the definitive hallmarks of nu-metal, the now-infamous mass of pop song remakes, which motivated the likes of Machine Head, Dope, and Alien Ant Farm to put their own spin on notable pop classics.

Prominent slots on both 1997's Warped Tour and 1998's Ozzfest gave Limp Bizkit further mainstream exposure, as did the unexpected popularity of "Faith," particularly on MTV and shows like *TRL*, which played its video on heavy rotation. But it's Limp Bizkit's addition to the Korn-founded 1998 Family Values Tour that truly set the band on the path to being the next big thing in nu-metal, and it wouldn't take long for its mosh-tailored sound to reach the apex of the charts. Issued just three weeks after Blink-182's *Enema of the State* set a new wave of pop-punk into motion, Limp Bizkit's second studio album, *Significant Other*, released on June 22, 1999, instantly took the music world by storm, debuting atop the US *Billboard* 200 with first-week sales totaling 643,874 units, a gargantuan number by anyone's standards.

Limp Bizkit had—for all the pros and cons—taken nu-metal to the next level, more than doubling the opening week sales of Korn's 1998 third studio album and first chart-topper on the US *Billboard* 200, *Follow the Leader*, which shipped an impressive 268,000 copies in its own right. Reviews for *Significant Other* were also more favorable compared with *Three Dollar Bill, Y'all*, with critics praising front man Fred Durst's performance, as exemplified by Sandy Masuo's 1999 review for the *Los Angeles Times*, which states, "Working his way through bitterness, fury, spite, desolation and disillusionment, he [Durst] not only delivers some of his strongest raps to date, but also sings convincingly."

By 1999, Durst had become the unofficial face of the scene, the signature red Yankees cap-wearing poster boy for a generation that grew up on a steady diet of equal parts hip-hop and metal. Durst personified the good, the bad, and the ugly of nu-metal more than any other individual, and his reckless attitude would soon lead to his—and the scene's—ruin. His lewd lyrics in "Nookie," the first single released from *Significant Other*, did little to change the views of those who called his writing sexist, while the record's fourth and final single, "Break Stuff," earned a reputation as a rowdy live favorite long before its release the following year. It was during the summer of 1999, though, that the song first made headlines, after Limp Bizkit's riotous set at Woodstock '99.

Unlike the definitive statement of the Flower Power generation, Woodstock '99 was anything but three days of peace and music, as the original 1969 festival is remembered. Everything that could have gone wrong did, and framed as the patsy for the myriad problems was the festival's uncontrollable hype man, Fred Durst. But before Limp Bizkit took to the stage on Saturday, July 24, tensions were already running high between the festivalgoers and the organizers. Poor planning and location scouting and a woeful lack of adequate sanitation facilities resulted in the festival ground's transformation into a cauldron of molten concrete and bodily fluids after temperatures at the former Griffiss Air Force Base in Rome, New York, soared to over 100°F.

Exacerbating the sweltering heat and hygiene issues was the spiraling cost of the festival's insufficient stock of concessions. Subcontracted vendors, who were able to charge whatever they desired, took advantage of the attendees—most notoriously by tripling the price of bottled water—throughout the festival's duration. Not even the free water stations provided much respite, as those waiting in line became so infuriated with the wasted hours spent queuing that they broke the water pipes for quicker access, inadvertently leading to an outbreak of trench foot and mouth. (In an inquiry after the fact, samples of the free drinking water were found to be contaminated with several bacteria, including E. coli, a common cause of severe infection and food poisoning.)

However, by far the most significant oversight was a deficiency of professional security officers—another cost-cutting measure imposed by the festival's organizers. Instead, Woodstock '99 entrusted the safety of its patrons—a reported 220,000 people—to inexperienced youngsters, many of whom exploited their duties (with allegations of theft, bribery, and sexual harassment from numerous in attendance) and saw the job as nothing more than a free ticket. Not only did this carelessness result in an incalculable amount of violence and vandalism, but sexual assaults were also rampant—a horrific consequence of the era's predatory frat-boy culture. Add all of the above together and it's no wonder Woodstock '99 was a disaster on every level.

Onstage, Woodstock '99—which was broadcast live as a pay-per-view event on MTV—was marred by foul incidents from the start of the festival's first full day: Friday, July 23. On the festival's main stage, the East Stage, obscenities like "Show your tits!" were repeatedly screamed at Sheryl Crow and Rosie Perez, the first of whom even accused one repulsive attendee of throwing excrement at her. The Offspring's Dexter Holland was struck by a beer bottle and later voiced his disgust with the disorderly crowd after seeing multiple women being groped while crowd surfing. Things over on the second stage, the West Stage, were just as bad, as Insane Clown Posse incited fighting among the unruly herd after hurling several beach balls taped with $100 bills into the crowd.

Though, the worst incident reported during Friday's proceedings happened back on the East Stage during Korn's otherwise exceptional set. Incidents of groping and sexual harassment were rife during Woodstock '99, but the legacy of Korn's concert was tarnished after a volunteer, David Schneider, alleged to have witnessed the gang rape of a young female before headliner Bush managed to close out what remained of the festival's first full day without further incident. (On July 28, 1999, just three days after the festival's end, an article published by *The Washington Post* reported four incidents of rape were being investigated by the police, and according to a 2021 article published by *Rolling Stone*, "Of the 44 people arrested at Woodstock '99, only one was charged with sexual assault.")

As Saturday dawned, the chaos resumed right from the get-go, as the East Stage was pelted with bottles during performances by Tragically Hip, Kid Rock, and Wyclef Jean. (The last two of whom, in an apparent act of solidarity, commanded the audience to cover the stage in a sea of bottles because of their disgust at the price of food and drink.) True to form, Kid Rock made additional references to the Clinton-Lewinsky scandal by demeaning Monica Lewinsky's part in the affair while, nauseatingly, celebrating President Clinton for his role. Alternative rock band Guster found it difficult over on the West Stage too, as its set was performed in front of an intimidating crowd that had little interest in the band's music and were, instead, waiting for their next opportunity to get into a brawl.

Even the '90s milquetoast jam band kings themselves, Dave Matthews Band, got in on the act by remarking on the sheer volume of topless women flashing them throughout its performance. Alanis Morissette, who followed Dave Matthews Band on the East Stage, was then—like every other female act that graced Woodstock '99—met with boos, jeers, and general apathy from those awaiting the festival's most eagerly anticipated act: Limp Bizkit. There was already a palpable sense of impending doom before Limp Bizkit took to the stage on the evening of Saturday, July 24. And soon after the band did, things really began to boil over. From this moment on, nu-metal became thought of as the biggest pariah in music, and its status had fumbled to a ruinous point of no return.

Looking more like a concert that had broken out in the middle of a riot than a peaceful evening of music and love, Limp Bizkit's performance was engulfed by an ocean of toxicity that worsened as the set went on. Moshing became increasingly violent and resulted in numerous injuries. Small buildings that surrounded the East Stage were torn down, and shredded parts were used to crowd surf by some in attendance. After Limp Bizkit's performance of "9 Teen 90 Nine," Durst was even approached by the festival's staff and asked to calm things down. That request, however, was disregarded by Durst, who told the crowd, "Don't let nobody get hurt, but I don't think you should mellow out. Mellowing out? That's what Alanis Morissette just had you motherfuckers do."

As unremarkable as those few words may seem in the grander scheme of things, that was all it took for things to turn really sour. Then, by the time Limp Bizkit guitarist Wes Borland struck the opening chords to "Break Stuff," all hell had officially broken loose. Durst's microphone was muted after the band finished the song while staff tried to intervene and help those needing medical attention. But with the sun slowly setting in the background, Durst wanted more and was desperate to get in on the action. After ignoring security's advice, Durst jumped into the crowd and surfed on a piece of broken plywood during the band's final song, "Faith," which ended with Durst being escorted offstage and informed of the crowd's destruction.

In another time and place, Durst's behavior may have been celebrated as an era-defining act of union between an artist and the fans, but in the aftermath of Woodstock '99 it became the deciding factor when the festival needed a fall guy to throw to the wolves. Further incidents of sexual assault were also reported to have taken place during Limp Bizkit's set, after which Rage Against the Machine and Metallica closed out day two. But one more day of chaos remained, and things were about to get much worse. By the time the Red Hot Chili Peppers drew the festival to a close on Sunday, July 25, the sight of Woodstock '99 had turned into a scene from a disaster movie, with bonfires raging, audio towers burning, and festivalgoers looting, vandalizing, and setting ablaze everything in sight.

As Woodstock '99 was being broadcast live on MTV, the violence and destruction was televised for the world to see. Even *TRL* host Carson Daly and *MTV News* correspondent Kurt Loder voiced their fears over the hostilities, leaving MTV no choice but to evacuate its entire crew. With an assist from nearby New York State Police troopers and other branches of law enforcement, things at the Griffiss Air Force Base finally started to settle down in the early hours of Monday morning. This, however, became the only period of calm the festival's organizers, original Woodstock cofounder Michael Lang and concert promoter John Scher, would feel before a storm of lawsuits and fines materialized over the following weeks and months. (As of 2025, Woodstock '99 remains the festival's latest edition.)

When everything is taken into consideration, it's clear Woodstock '99 was a catastrophe long before Limp Bizkit took to the stage. And I know Fred Durst didn't exactly help matters by being too caught up in his own private party, but it was spineless of the festival's organizers, the media, and fellow musicians to try to scapegoat Durst and put the blame on Limp Bizkit's shoulders. (In the aftermath of Woodstock '99, both Korn's Jonathan Davis and Rage Against the Machine's Tom Morello publicly blamed Limp Bizkit for its role in the festival's downfall; however, in more recent years, both have softened their stance and have even toured with Limp Bizkit, ending any animosity between the groups.)

The actual blame for the festival's troubles lies in the egregious negligence of its organizers, whose lack of accountability—even after all these years—remains a slap in the face to the victims of the weekend's horrors. As history attests, the 1969 festival will be forever celebrated as a historic event in the story of popular music. But Woodstock '99 will only ever be remembered as the definitive precautionary tale on how not to organize a festival. (I strongly endorse both HBO's 2021 documentary film *Woodstock 99: Peace, Love, and Rage* and Netflix's 2022 three-part docuseries *Trainwreck: Woodstock '99* for a more visual documentation of the festival's downfall and John Scher's distasteful attempts to rationalize the weekend's offenses.)

It's not often that a relatively new style of music hits both its peak and rock-bottom in the same year; in fact, I can't recall it ever happening anywhere else. But that kind of roller-coaster experience is precisely what

1999 proved to be for nu-metal. In addition to Limp Bizkit's monstrously successful *Significant Other*, Static-X and Crazy Town emerged with platinum-selling debuts, as did Slipknot, arguably the most important and acclaimed metal band from the past twenty-five years, which fittingly chose Ross Robinson as the man to distill the band's chaotic energy into its iconic self-titled debut record. New studio albums by Machine Head, Coal Chamber, and Korn also sold well and rank among the best-selling of their careers.

But while Limp Bizkit's follow-up to *Significant Other*, 2000's *Chocolate Starfish and the Hot Dog Flavored Water*, continued nu-metal's commercial growth in the early part of the new millennium, debuting atop the US *Billboard* 200 and selling over one million copies in its first week alone (only the seventh album to have done so at the time), the damage to the scene's public reputation had already been done—and its standing among fellow musicians never fully recovered. Nu-metal's originator, Korn, immediately began to reject the label, with Jonathan Davis saying in a 2019 interview with *NME* that the "scene was full of misogynistic, opportunistic dickhead jocks. The sort of people who'd be bullying me at school if they weren't supporting my band at shows."

Nu-metal progenitor Rage Against the Machine went the extra step and openly mocked bands like Limp Bizkit, with bassist Tim Commerford being quoted in a 2015 interview with *Rolling Stone* as saying, "I do apologize for Limp Bizkit. I really do. I feel really bad that we inspired such bullshit." Record labels didn't help much either, as they tried to cash in on nu-metal's profitability with a derivative batch of copycats that had more in common with flash-in-the-pan boy bands like LFO and O-Town. Then, by the time Bowling for Soup released the music video to its 2002 hit song, "Girl All the Bad Guys Want," in which the band spoofs the videos of Limp Bizkit and Staind, nu-metal had become a full-on joke, and its mainstream appeal was a shadow of its glory days just a few years prior.

It's a shame the cloud of Woodstock '99 hangs over the heads of Limp Bizkit with such notoriety because its legacy as one of the best-selling acts of the era seems to have been forgotten. I could easily sit here and claim Limp Bizkit was simply a product of the time and not elaborate any further, but that wouldn't be justifiable given the climate in which the band prospered. In her 2018 book, *90s Bitch: Media, Culture, and the Failed Promise of Gender Equality*, author Allison Yarrow says, "I loved my 90s childhood. But it wasn't until returning to this decade as an adult that I came to see how mainstream 90s narratives in media and society promoted sexism and exploited girlhood." I'm a child of the 1990s, too, and it's only in adulthood that I've also discovered the extent to which I was oblivious to the decade's seediness.

Pop culture outright normalized misogyny during the '90s, and the US isn't the only country at fault for much of the era's backward gender politics. Before the internet gave the likes of Andrew Tate an unfiltered platform to spew his malignant manosphere bigotry, UK lad mags like *Loaded* and *FHM* encouraged a degenerate mentality within young heterosexual men and threatened to upend years of progress toward gender equality. But what allegedly started as an ironic position against political correctness quickly became an ugly reflection of the time's relationship with women when, in 1999, as part of an unethical

*Significant Other* by Limp Bizkit
Courtesy of Flip Records and Interscope Records

guerrilla marketing campaign by *FHM*, a nude photograph of Scottish TV personality Gail Porter was projected on the Houses of Parliament without her consent.

This kind of misogyny was a symptom of a bigger, more sinister problem—one from which many facets of entertainment, unfortunately, reaped the benefits. Admittedly, I don't think Fred Durst's lyrics to "Eat You Alive" are likely to be retroactively awarded the Nobel Prize in Literature, but are his words any more problematic than those found in "Run for Your Life" by the Beatles or "Brown Sugar" by the Rolling Stones? I'll let you be the judge. Some things aren't meant to last forever; maybe nu-metal is just one of them. Its downfall was no different from the demise of disco or glam metal before it. They all reflected the time and place in which they were created and were all abandoned by their audience after the music had stagnated to a cycle of diminishing returns.

As much as I'll always have a fondness for the style and the music it birthed, nu-metal thrived in a highly toxic time, and a portion of its audience—the type of people who confuse physical aggression with emotional strength—reflected that. Allison Yarrow summarizes her thoughts on the matter by concluding, "In the end, the 1990s didn't advance women and girls; rather, the decade was marked by a shocking, accelerating effort to subordinate them." Nevertheless, no artist controls what kind of audience latches onto their music. But a song no longer belongs to the artist once it's let out into the world, and unfortunately, lyrics can be co-opted and distorted to fit any individual's specific agenda. Sadly, that's one thing that will never change.

"Born in the U.S.A." was written by Bruce Springsteen as a critique of the Vietnam War and America's treatment of veterans upon their return home but can be warped into militant nationalist propaganda when put in the hands of the wrong politician. Limp Bizkit's "Break Stuff" can be read as an anthem of liberation, a cathartic exorcism for pent-up negative energy. Performed in front of thousands of unruly hooligans who couldn't care less about the safety of those around them, though, it becomes a license for human-rights-violating behavior and a shameful call to wreak as much havoc as possible. (At Lollapalooza 2021, Durst introduced the song by asserting to the audience, "Let me make this clear: this is not Woodstock '99. Fuck all that bullshit.")

Given how much time has passed since Woodstock '99, lad mags, and celebrity sex tapes had any notable cultural relevance, I'd like to think we're in a much better place in this post-#MeToo era. But are we really? Answer me this: Were you one of the reported sixty-five million people who switched on Netflix to watch a live boxing match between a former heavyweight world champion and a YouTuber on November 15, 2024? Maybe you didn't realize that said former heavyweight world champion, who was reportedly paid $20 million for the fight, spent three years in prison after being found guilty of rape in 1992. Maybe you didn't realize multiple women have also accused his opponent of sexual assault; he was apparently paid $40 million.

Maybe if we all looked up from our phones for more than a minute and questioned how the forty-seventh president of the United States was allowed to reenter office despite being found liable for sexual abuse and defamation in 2023, we'd realize not much has changed since 1999 after all . . .

*CHAPTER 8*
# Smells (Kinda) Like Teen Spirit

August 24, 1999, saw the arrival of yet another pop sensation, Christina Aguilera, whose self-titled debut studio album immediately put her on par with her fellow *The All-New Mickey Mouse Club* alumna Britney Spears, debuting atop the US *Billboard* 200 with opening-week sales of 253,000 copies and going on to sell over fourteen million units worldwide. Yet shortly after Aguilera's debut, a somewhat familiar sound from earlier in the decade—albeit less raw and more commercially minded—returned to the top of the charts and kickstarted a second wave of post-grunge dominance. It was during the original grunge movement's decline in the mid-1990s, however, that the offshoot had first found worldwide recognition—and no shortage of snotty-nosed cynicism from those who championed grunge's revolutionary impact.

Perhaps the last great movement of the MTV Generation, grunge stood in direct opposition to its glam metal adversaries with an abruptly conflicting sound and aesthetic. In explicitly reflecting Gen X's fragmented outlook on the era's societal problems, bands like Soundgarden, Nirvana, Alice in Chains, and Pearl Jam all unambiguously rejected the hackneyed yuppie indulgences of the 1980s by presenting a more authentic take on everything from sociopolitical issues and environmentalism to drug abuse and self-destruction. (In a 2022 interview with *The New York Times*, Pearl Jam front man Eddie Vedder said of glam metal and, specifically,

Mötley Crüe, "I hated it. I hated how it made the fellas look. I hated how it made the women look. It felt so vacuous.")

If the philosophies of the grunge movement don't sound particularly new or radical for the time, it's because they weren't. But in merging the themes and DIY ethos of hardcore punk innovator Black Flag with the doomy viscosity of sludge metal forerunners the Melvins, grunge became the antithesis of Reaganomics excess, bringing alternative music back to its humble roots. However, what was originally an underground subculture—primarily in the rain-soaked, light-deprived Pacific Northwest region of Seattle, Washington—quickly became a mainstream attraction after the "Seattle sound" outgrew the financial limitations of famed independent record label Sub Pop and saw the genre's biggest act, Nirvana, signing with a major label, DGC Records, founded in 1990 by David Geffen.

Between 1991 and 1995, an abundance of critically acclaimed and commercially successful records made grunge the most popular form of alternative music of the time. But the 1994 death of Nirvana leader and reluctant voice of Gen X Kurt Cobain became an underlying factor in the movement's collapse and eventual fade to black toward the end of the decade. By the mid-1990s, the music industry had marketed and exploited everything for which the original grunge movement stood. Grunge's antimaterialist stance on clothing, for example, became warped into high-street fashion, turning everyday flannel shirts into a trendy accessory. The scene's unique blend of hardcore punk and heavy metal also became decidedly more commercial—a direct result of major-label funding.

As record labels looked to rinse every last dollar out of grunge's dwindling popularity, the first wave of post-grunge bands emerged. Despite indifferent reactions from mainstream critics, bands like Live, Candlebox, and Collective Soul all saw significant chart success in the mid-'90s via a sound that was conspicuously similar to grunge but contained only trace amounts of its authenticity. Former Nirvana drummer Dave Grohl started Foo Fighters shortly after his previous group's disbandment, with its self-titled debut record—initially envisioned as a solo project—launching a little over a year after Cobain's passing. But it was over on my side of the pond where the first wave of post-grunge found its original whipping boys in UK-based Nirvana worshipper Bush.

Formed in London in 1992, Bush immediately drew considerable attention—most of it negative—from the US media due to the band's similar sound to Nirvana and the like. The origins of Bush front man Gavin Rossdale's lyrical influences, specifically in antisexist songs like "Testosterone," can be traced to the Cobain-penned song "Polly," as can the juxtaposition between Bush's soft, jangly verses and fuzzily muscular choruses—a classic instrumental trait of grunge—which numerous critics noted at the time. One in particular, Matt Diehl, called Bush "the most successful and shameless mimics of Nirvana's music" in his *Rolling Stone*-published review of the band's 1996 second studio album, *Razorblade Suitcase*, a US *Billboard* 200 chart-topper.

During the time of *Razorblade Suitcase*'s success, the first wave of post-grunge reached its zenith, with Live, Candlebox, Collective Soul, and Bush all struggling to attain the same level of prominence thereafter. But as the first wave of post-grunge started to lose popularity, a second wave appeared with an identity that not only shifted further away from the grunge's anti-rock star sensibilities but also added a sprinkle of cock rock swagger to the mix, finding just as much inspiration in the rakish figures of Jim Morrison and Robert Plant as Kurt Cobain and Eddie Vedder. One such act, Nickelback, surfaced in 1996 with its little-heard debut studio album, *Curb*, but it wouldn't be until the 2000s that the band discovered the full extent of its commercial reach.

The first band to truly push the second wave of post-grunge into uncharted territory was Creed, whose 1997 debut studio album, *My Own Prison*, injected the alternative scene with a dose of ideology that was previously rebuked: faith. Songs critical of religion have been commonplace in popular music for decades, prompting compositions by everyone from Monty Python to Pearl Jam. John Lennon's views on organized religion's hypocrisies, for instance, were a recurring theme throughout his solo work released after the Beatles' breakup. Likewise, grunge artists have never been shy about their beliefs—or lack thereof. Especially notable was Soundgarden's 1991 song "Jesus Christ Pose," released as the first single from the band's third studio album, *Badmotorfinger*, which caused quite the stir on MTV.

Soundgarden's controversial music video for "Jesus Christ Pose," directed by Eric Zimmerman, hasn't been played in full on MTV since 1991; this is because when it was originally aired on the network, many viewers deemed its striking imagery—including a crucified lady, an apparent allusion to history's endless persecution of women—anti-Christian. But as allegorical as the symbolism in the "Jesus Christ Pose" music video may be, the 1990s was replete with artists who were more forthright in their views, including Marilyn Manson, which has openly challenged religion's power structures since its 1994 debut, perhaps most famously in the chorus to the band's response to Columbine's aftermath, "The Fight Song," in which its namesake singer screams in despair at his views on religion's alleged societal control.

Creed, unlike Marilyn Manson, went in the opposite direction, using theological imagery as metaphors in many of its biggest hits. Although he survived an upbringing scarred by a religiously abusive stepfather, Creed front man Scott Stapp has worn his Christian faith on his sleeve for the entirety of his career. This has led to accusations of pushing an agenda from many in the industry, despite Stapp's assertion that his lyrics serve no such purpose. Writing in *The Washington Post* in 1999, Mark Jenkins said, "Creed is something more profound than a mere commercial phenomenon. The biblical imagery of singer Scott Stapp's lyrics got Creed typed as Christian rock by early listeners, and the band's denial of any religious objective has unsettled some of its more fervent fans."

Creed illustrated its various influences from the outset with its debut studio album, *My Own Prison*, recorded for only $6,000. The music blended elements of grunge and thrash metal, a favorite of the band's lead guitarist and main composer, Mark Tremonti, whose later work with Alter Bridge—one of the most acclaimed bands of the twenty-first century—gave him a stage to further showcase his widely acknowledged technical expertise. Stapp's lyrics throughout *My Own Prison* include themes of faith, rebellion, sin, and personal responsibility, evident perhaps no more so than on the record's titular lead single, which became the band's breakthrough hit after peaking at number two on the US *Billboard* Mainstream Rock chart on November 8, 1997.

As with the first wave of post-grunge, critics weren't particularly kind to *My Own Prison*, but after a slow start, the record began to outsell its previous weekly tally week after week, peaking at number twenty-two on the US *Billboard* 200—more than a year after its debut—on May 2, 1998. Proving to be the pivotal turning point in Creed's success, 1998 saw the band go from strength to strength. *My Own Prison*'s third single, "What's This Life For," peaked atop the US *Billboard* Mainstream Rock chart on September 19, 1998, staying there for an additional five weeks. The song was also featured in *Halloween H20: 20 Years Later*, the franchise's seventh installment and first—of now several—to bring back series heroine Jamie Lee Curtis after a seventeen-year absence.

Additional songs, such as "Bound and Tied" and a cover of Alice Cooper's "I'm Eighteen," were featured in *Dead Man on Campus* and *The Faculty*, respectively, enhancing Creed's continued mainstream appeal, and helping *My Own Prison* to over six million sales in the US by August 26, 2002. The record's meteoric rise to six-times-platinum can be attributed to many factors, but only one element is responsible for Creed's sudden mainstream saturation: the overwhelming success of the band's eleven-times-platinum second studio album. Like any act smart enough to ride the wave of fame, Creed was quick to capitalize on its newfound success in the lead-up to *Human Clay*'s 1999 release, including having the (dis)honor of playing the penultimate main stage set at Woodstock '99.

Thankfully, nothing unpleasant was reported to have taken place, a minor miracle given what happened elsewhere. Instead, Creed's concert is best remembered for the band's three-song alliance with Doors guitarist Robby Krieger, who joined them to perform two of his band's classics, "Roadhouse Blues" and "Riders on the Storm," and a rendition of "What's This Life For" that closed Creed's show. Given the awful happenings throughout that fateful weekend in July, Creed's performance with Krieger has been understandably overshadowed in the decades since. But it nonetheless serves as a reminder of what Woodstock '99 could have been—a celebration of music both old and new, commemorated by generations past and present.

In contrast to many bands that performed at Woodstock '99, Creed walked away relatively unscathed (apart from the opinions of those who'd mocked the band from the start) and was primed to make the most out of its exposure to the hundreds of thousands of people in attendance.

Nearly a month to the day after Creed's performance at Woodstock '99, the band released its first single from *Human Clay*, "Higher," which not only climbed to the top of both the US *Billboard* Modern Rock Tracks and Mainstream Rock charts, staying atop the latter for a (since surpassed) record seventeen weeks, but also became its first single to chart inside the Hot 100's top ten. ("Higher" finally reached gold certification on May 19, 2019, and has since been certified two-times-platinum.)

Perhaps an indication of just how far the band had come in the two years since its debut, expectations were at an all-time high in the countdown to *Human Clay*'s arrival, but few people could've predicted just how significant that record was to become. Released on September 28, 1999, *Human Clay* debuted at number one on the US *Billboard* 200 chart after shifting 315,000 units in its first week, ultimately becoming not only Creed's most successful album but also one of the best-selling records in US chart history. With a monster success surpassing even the most optimistic projections, Creed found itself on top of the music world despite critics' unrelenting bewilderment.

In his 1999 review for the *Los Angeles Times*, Marc Weingarten says of *Human Clay*, "Much of the album is grunge twice-removed. The songs sound less like knockoffs of such standard-bearers as Pearl Jam and Alice in Chains than they do facsimiles of Seven Mary Three and Stone Temple Pilots" (although, rather backhandedly, he does concede in the same review that "Like Krispy Kreme doughnuts, Creed has concocted a winning formula and dares not deviate from it, lest it result in lost market share"). Though not entirely invalid, this sarcastic assessment of Creed's music was shared by many critics at the time (both *Entertainment Weekly* and *Rolling Stone* expressed similar sentiments) who could never bring themselves to provide the band with any sincere credit despite its accomplishments.

Conversely, audiences—both those of faith and nonbelievers—have taken to Creed's music like a duck to water, making the band one of the most successful acts of the MTV2 Generation. By the end of 1999, *Human Clay* was already approaching three-times-platinum after shifting close to three million units in the US alone. By July 16, 2001, the record had sold over ten million copies in the US, putting the band among an exclusive group of artists with a diamond-certified album. (*Human*

*Clay*'s most recent certification, eleven-times-platinum, was awarded on January 29, 2004.) Creed's biggest hit, "With Arms Wide Open," released as the third single from *Human Clay* on April 12, 2000, peaked at number one on the US *Billboard* Hot 100 on November 11, 2000.

In hitting the top position on the US *Billboard* Hot 100, Creed became one of only a handful of rock artists to have achieved that feat in the last twenty-five years, arguably setting the stage for Canadian post-grunge flag bearer Nickelback, whose own mainstream breakthrough, "How You Remind Me," likewise peaked atop the same chart in late 2001. However much corporately mandated, the second wave of post-grunge's success at its peak had surpassed that of the first wave and was commercially—at least, if not foundationally—on equal footing with the original movement's popularity. (On February 21, 2001, "With Arms Wide Open" also won the Grammy Award for Best Rock Song, earning Creed its first—and thus far only—win from three nominations.)

Following the success of *Human Clay*, the second wave of post-grunge saw a drastic upsurge in popularity over the next few years, a payoff for both greener and more established acts. In addition to Nickelback, bands like Staind, 3 Doors Down, Puddle of Mudd, and Seether all released a stack of RIAA-certified albums and singles in the early 2000s. The

*Human Clay* by Creed
Courtesy of Wind-up Records

second wave's traction showed no signs of slowing down in the mid-to-late '00s either, as such bands as Breaking Benjamin, Shinedown, Three Days Grace, and Hinder achieved comparable commercial success. And now, over two decades after *Human Clay* initially prevailed despite all the naysayers, post-grunge finds itself in a rather unusual position: people are actually praising it out in the open!

On November 17, 2023, *Vice* published an article called: "Hear Me Out: Creed Are Finally Cool." Its author, Magdalene Taylor, starts by saying, "When you were young, if you had any thoughts about Creed at all, it was likely that they were corny. They were overly earnest, vaguely worship-y, bordering on Christian rock." This is where the article takes a left turn, though, and she goes on to argue how the simplicity in Creed's sincerity has been lost in our present climate. And she's right, given how today's cultural wasteland promotes the weaponization of diversity through anti-egalitarian clickbait. Honestly, I always heard Scott Stapp's lyrics as more metaphorical than spiritual, but maybe that's because I'm not religious.

Personally, I can't grasp how someone could possibly have faith in institutions that have tried to hush thousands of cases detailing sexual abuse and adoption fraud dating back hundreds of years, but who am I to judge what—or what not—someone chooses to believe? Individual beliefs are none of my business, and so long as they're not used for nefarious purposes, I have no right to discriminate against anyone's convictions. Writers have forever been told to write about what they know, and Scott Stapp did just that. Whether overtly religious or not, Creed has always tried to connect with the world via a vulnerability and appreciation for life itself.

That earnestness may have been met with widespread cynicism in the '90s, but now, twenty-five years later, as Magdalene Taylor says at the end of her article, "Perhaps we took it for granted before, but Creed has always welcomed us in that embrace." I don't know about you, but if spreading positivity—among a sea of toxicity—is the kind of legacy for which Creed will be remembered, then I think the band should be proud for communicating its message out to the world.

*CHAPTER 9*

# The Heavier the Music, the Nicer the People: A Conversation with Acclaimed Music Biographer and Magazine Editor Joel McIver

Having spent over twenty-five years as a journalist, author, and magazine editor, Joel McIver has earned a reputation as one of the leading voices in the music sphere, regularly appearing on TV and radio as an expert in rock and metal. Having authored or coauthored over thirty books, including the biographies of some of heavy music's biggest names, Joel's knowledge and credibility go far beyond that of a casual fan, and it was a treat to sit down with him to chat about his career, his earliest influences, and his thoughts on alternative music's ever-changing landscape.

**Jon Sheasby:** As one of the leading music biographers of the past twenty-five years, authoring books on everyone from Ice Cube [*Ice Cube: Attitude*] to Rob Zombie [*Sinister Urge: The Life and Times of Rob Zombie*], was it your love of music or reading that came first?

**Joel McIver:** A great question. I would think reading probably. I was a nerd at school; I always wanted to be a writer and was good at it. Then I got massively into music in my early teens. Actually, earlier than that, because my parents used to have quite a few cool LPs by people like Jimi Hendrix and stuff like that. So probably reading and writing first, then music, and then obviously the two fell together.

**Jon Sheasby:** Who were some authors and musicians that first inspired you as a kid?

**Joel McIver:** Authors is easy because I was a sci-fi nerd. I just read Isaac Asimov and fantasy fiction by [J. R. R.] Tolkien and all the obvious stuff like that. Musicwise, my dad had an early compilation by the Beatles, which you can still find, called *A Collection of Beatles Oldies*.

**Jon Sheasby:** I've got that record right in front of me!

**Joel McIver:** You know it, do you? [Laughs.] I can't remember when it came out [1966], but it was just a collection of Beatles songs, which I absolutely fell in love with at about ten or eleven. My mom had a Deep Purple side project [1974's *The Butterfly Ball and the Grasshopper's Feast*] by Roger Glover, the bass player, and I used to love that when I was five or six. By the age of about twelve, I got into Duran Duran. I was really into all that nonsense because it was big at the time, and I loved the songs and the bass playing. Soft Cell was massive for me. I had the first Soft Cell album [1981's *Non-Stop Erotic Cabaret*]. I've interviewed Marc Almond several times over the years, and he's a huge hero. And then the metal thing came along. I had a kind of sudden conversion—quite late, actually—at the age of seventeen. A mate of mine played me *Master of Puppets*, Metallica's third album, which was giant for me. It just changed everything. I knew heavy metal existed, but I thought it was all rather tragic, spandex kind of stuff. [Laughs.] And then I realized that it really wasn't. I got into thrash metal massively on the back of that, and then a bit later, it's death metal, and then on we go. Then I rediscovered all the classic stuff: Black Sabbath, Judas Priest, Motörhead, Iron Maiden, etc. That was all by the time I was about seventeen, eighteen.

**Jon Sheasby:** You've seen the metal world evolve through thrash, glam, nu-metal, and everything in between, and you've written about all the above in your books. So what are your thoughts, as a fan, on seeing the changes the scene's gone through in your lifetime?

**Joel McIver:** Well, I've been very impressed by its longevity. It's gone through all those changes, and yet it still keeps going. And that says to me that there's something about it which is sort of necessary. People don't just enjoy metal; they live it. I've thought about this and discussed it in great detail with various people. So one of the theories that I've pursued, especially with people like Max Cavalera when I did his book [*My Bloody Roots: From Sepultura to Soulfly and Beyond*], is that metal is somewhat of a haven, especially for young men who lack a father or lack some other kind of male presence in their lives, because it gives them that. That's one element of it that indicates to me that metal isn't just a bit of entertainment. It's actually quite existentially important. So there's that element of it. And then the other thing is the tribal aspect, which is obvious. I was talking to a mate of mine about this yesterday, actually. He said, "Nowadays, you don't see kids dressed in a particular way that indicates what musical tribe they belong to."

**Jon Sheasby:** Sure, yeah.

**Joel McIver:** And I said, "Well, actually, you do, but it's only the metalheads as far as I can tell." You can spot the metal, emo, and goth kids a mile off. But as far as I know, and I could be wrong, there aren't any other tribes, as it were, who dress in a particular way that's an allegiance to the music they like. So when I was a kid in the '80s, there was a massive mod revival.

**Jon Sheasby:** Of course.

**Joel McIver:** Yeah, you'll know about this. It was massive. And all the kids dressed in the mod gear, and then you'd get your pop kids who dressed like Duran Duran with all that nonsense, and you could tell what people listened to. But I think only really heavy music fans dress like

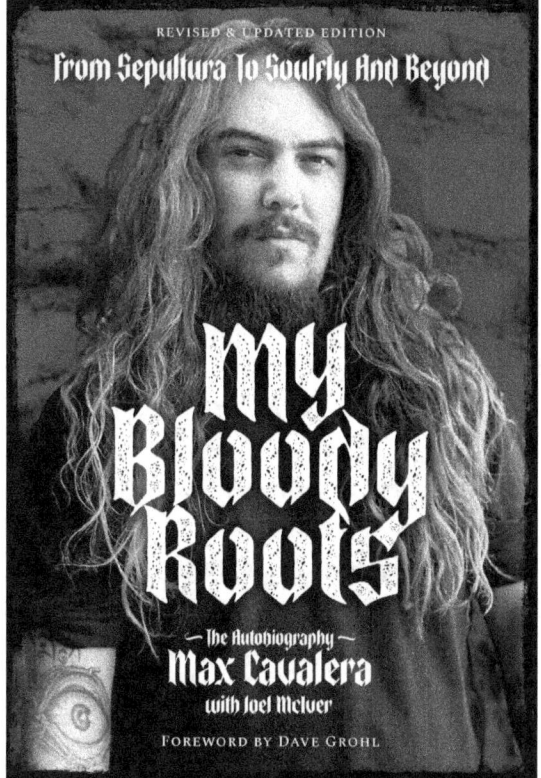

*My Bloody Roots: From Sepultura to Soulfly and Beyond*
by Max Cavalera and Joel McIver
Courtesy of Jawbone Press

heavy music fans nowadays, and I think that's indicative of the music's particular strength.

**Jon Sheasby:** Are there any specific metal subgenres that appeal to you more than others?

**Joel McIver:** I tend not to listen to midtempo metal. I love thrash metal, death metal, and black metal. If I'm gonna listen to metal music, it's basically because it's fast. It gives me an adrenaline surge. But that's not to say that I only listen to fast metal all day every day, right? I listen to an awful lot of other music too. Pop, country, folk, classical, funk, jazz, soul, R&B, reggae, etc. Everything. I listen to it.

**Jon Sheasby:** Uh-huh.

**Joel McIver:** And that's clearly not all about the speed, is it? So metal has always been a fast thing for me. Those three subgenres: thrash, death, and black.

**Jon Sheasby:** Correct me if I'm wrong, but I think I'm right in saying your first published book was *Extreme Metal*, and your third was *Nu-Metal: The Next Generation of Rock and Punk*, right?

**Joel McIver:** That's correct, yeah. The idea was that the second one followed on from the first. I did a Slipknot book [*Slipknot: Unmasked*] in between. I'm sort of in two minds about those books. I wrote my first book—the *Extreme Metal* book—when I was twenty-eight, twenty-nine. And it isn't great. I don't exactly cringe when I look back, but I made too many jokes, and it's not very well researched, and it's all pre-internet. So it's kind of crap, but it's not terrible. The same is true of the nu-metal book, which I slightly look back on and cringe because nu-metal is so cheesy now when you look at it. And even as I wrote it in '01 going into '02, it was on its way out a little bit already. So, it was slightly out of time. But they were fun to do, actually. And they got me rolling as an author. So yeah, no complaints. But I don't think I really got going as an author until I was on book four [*Ice Cube: Attitude*] or five [*Erykah Badu: The First Lady of Neo-Soul*].

**Jon Sheasby:** I'm referencing those two books in particular because I think it's interesting how a number of extreme bands embraced the nu-metal sound of the '90s and one in particular, Sepultura, commercially benefited from the stylistic change brought about after Korn's 1994 debut. Knowing that you cowrote Max Cavalera's autobiography, what are your thoughts on the bands whose styles shifted during that era?

**Joel McIver:** Some did. There weren't that many, but some did. I take your point about Sepultura. That's one hundred percent true. I'm not sure there was this giant movement of extreme bands turning nu-metal.

**Jon Sheasby:** Slayer put out that one record [1998's *Diabolus in Musica*], and Machine Head [1999's *The Burning Red* and 2001's *Supercharger*] did too.

**Joel McIver:** And then you had Rage Against the Machine and stuff like that. It's an interesting one. Good point. See, Max is a really good mate of mine. So since I've become friends with him, I don't have any judgmental thoughts about that particular thing. But at the time, because I was quite young and I was into my thrash, I was like, "What the fuck, man? Why are they slowing down?" [Laughs.] Whining, like, you know? So basically, what I know now is that in the case of Sepultura, they wanted to slow down and play more groovy stuff. They got Ross Robinson on board to give them that sound, and it worked really, really well. And *Roots* sold tons of copies. So yeah, at the time, I didn't really like it. Now I totally get it and like it. I would still rather listen to *Chaos A.D.* [Sepultura's fifth studio album] or something like that, something that's a bit more speedy. But I look back now and realize it made perfect sense for them to do it. That was just their next move. That was their next step. It was a brave, creative decision that paid off for them.

**Jon Sheasby:** And as you've interviewed hundreds of musicians from that time, is that sort of ambivalence towards that period something you've heard often, or have more artists embraced it over the years?

**Joel McIver:** One or two have regretted their decisions and privately regretted that stuff. Will they come out and say it, though, in public? [Laughs.]

**Jon Sheasby:** I think Kerry King from Slayer said he's regretful of that time, but a couple of other members have come out and said that they enjoyed the music they made and thought it was the most experimental Slayer's ever been.

**Joel McIver:** So what happened there was that Jeff Hanneman did most of the songwriting because Kerry stepped away. He wasn't really in the mood, I think. So Jeff, I think, was more influenced by that time, and he liked his moody, slower, grim-sounding stuff. The only full-on nu-metal song is "Stain of Mind," but it doesn't have a DJ even then. It just has that one riff, which Korn used in "Blind" and Coal Chamber used in "Loco." I can't stand that song ["Stain of Mind"], but fortunately, they didn't stick with it very long. I think it's just really that one song. *Diabolus in Musica* has some great stuff on it, though. They didn't completely give up on the thrash stuff, which was quite brave whenever that one came out. In 1998, was it?

**Jon Sheasby:** Yes.

**Joel McIver:** I interviewed Jon Bon Jovi around 2000 and said something like "Are you under pressure to change your sound ever? Like, you know, update it for the modern audience?" And he said, "What, you mean, like, get a DJ and then go nu-metal?" [Laughs.] And I said, "Well, no, that's not what I meant, actually." But it's interesting that it was clearly on his mind—the nu-metal sound—which was kind of interesting. I wasn't expecting that at all. But it was everywhere at the time. You couldn't get away from it. It wasn't all bad. Some of the nu-metal scene was quite good. Some of those songs by Linkin Park and Limp Bizkit are quite a lot of fun when you've had a few beers. But it was so image driven, which was depressing.

**Jon Sheasby:** It's quite funny to hear you talk about nu-metal from your point of view because I grew up with it, and it was the first type of heavy music I was ever introduced to. Limp Bizkit was my gateway into all metal, and I still love it despite all its obvious flaws.

**Joel McIver:** You gotta remember, I was nearly thirty, right? I suppose I was only twenty-three when *Korn* came out, but I was nearing thirty by the time nu-metal got massive. Because, honestly, so many bands were doing it, changing their look, and it was mental how popular it was. I can only attribute it to record companies deciding that nu-metal was the next big thing, so they decided to assemble a Backstreet Boys of nu-metal, gave them all seven-string guitars, got them to look aggressively into the camera, and then make a load of money. And they did! [Laughs.]

**Jon Sheasby:** [Laughs.] Absolutely.

**Joel McIver:** And, weirdly, I'm not really against all that. If you're a record company and want to make a ton of money, then be clever about it. But loads of those bands couldn't make it because they didn't have the songs, which led to a lot of otherwise fairly talented musicians just being completely ignored. There were just too many of them, and the way it looked got ridiculous. And while we're on the subject, you might have been going to ask me this, but it's blown my mind that it's so big now.

**Jon Sheasby:** Especially among young women too, with the likes of Poppy and Wargasm leading the revival. It's come back in a big, big way.

**Joel McIver:** Right? So my kids love all that stuff, and, to them, it's their version of classic rock. It blows my mind. [Laughs.] And the longevity of that music has very much surprised me. Limp Bizkit is still playing arenas, which kills me. Slipknot, they're a bit of a different phenomenon entirely because they transcended that sound, and I'm really proud of them for doing what they've done. They've got massive, and their music's so extreme, negative, and massively misanthropic. It had no right to be this big, and yet it is. So, the nu-metal scene has unexpectedly lived on.

**Jon Sheasby:** Regarding Limp Bizkit and nu-metal in general, I'd love to get your thoughts on the events of Woodstock '99. Back then, Limp Bizkit was just one of several popular bands accused of promoting misogyny within its lyrics, but nobody could've foreseen what eventually happened at Woodstock '99 and the backlash against the band in the festival's aftermath. Does nu-metal and bands like Limp Bizkit have any culpability in the era's toxicity, and do you think we're in danger of history repeating itself today given the popularity of the rhetoric expressed by Andrew Tate and the "red pill" community?

**Joel McIver:** I think what you had there [Woodstock '99] was a situation where you had a very inflammatory front man [Fred Durst] who did what he always did, right? Asking the crowd to smash things and stuff. It was provocative and arguably a bit dangerous, but it was in no way misogynistic. You can't blame Fred Durst for being Fred Durst. As for the assaults that took place, whether that was down to the era or a bunch of absolute morons in the crowd who thought it was appropriate, I don't blame Fred Durst or nu-metal's popularity for any of that. I don't know every single song by Limp Bizkit or every single lyric, but I don't remember there being many negative references to women. I think that was a much bigger problem in hip-hop, to be honest. And I think it's worse today, with the Andrew Tate phenomenon and everything happening now. It needs sorting out. A lot of young men need to be appropriately educated, and they need to understand that it's categorically wrong to be the dickheads they're being towards women.

**Jon Sheasby:** I couldn't agree more. On a lighter note, I can't help but notice that whenever I walk through any town or city today, all the skinny jeans and V-necks have gone, and they've been replaced by baggy jeans and oversized T-shirts, and people of all ages are once more dressing like they're in a nu-metal band from the early 2000s.

**Joel McIver:** I know, right? But the skinny jeans will be back. The skinny jeans will be back. It's funny: every time trousers become small, and then they're big again, and suddenly it seems like the coolest thing ever. And then you get to my age, and you don't give a fuck about that anymore. [Laughs.] It's an interesting phenomenon. The wheel of fashion.

**Jon Sheasby:** Have you ever received feedback from any artists you've chronicled in your work?

**Joel McIver:** One or two. Usually, I think, it's always been positive. Maybe a couple of people might've said, "Oh, you got this fact wrong." "Yeah, thanks for doing the book. Appreciate it. But you got this fact wrong." Which is fine. That's just regular journalistic diligence. I can't think of anyone who's got in touch and said, "You did a bad job on us," fortunately.

**Jon Sheasby:** How was it, then, shifting from writing from your point of view to cowriting biographies with rock and metal legends like Glenn Hughes [*Deep Purple and Beyond: Scenes from the Life of a Rock Star*], David Ellefson [*My Life with Deth: Discovering Meaning in a Life of Rock & Roll*], and the aforementioned Max Cavalera? How did that line of work come about?

**Joel McIver:** Well, that was a deliberate move on my part. I wanted to get into that. I think I'd already done twenty books or something of my own, and when you've done all that journalism and met them all, the obvious thing is to connect with these people and make it official rather than just writing your own stuff. It's been a really enjoyable experience, and it's a whole different ball game because they have magic address books, right? So Dave Grohl will do the foreword to Max's book, and Alice Cooper will do the foreword to Ellefson's book. I've really enjoyed that, and I'm in touch with loads of those people. I wholly recommend it if you're interested in doing that. It's great. It's a great thing to do.

**Jon Sheasby:** The first book I ever read of yours, actually, was Glenn Hughes's autobiography because I'm a massive fan of him and all the periods of his career. I love that book.

**Joel McIver:** Cool. That turned out really well. It turned out so well, that book.

**Jon Sheasby:** Was Glenn's book your idea?

**Joel McIver:** Yeah, that was my idea. I had interviewed him for *Bass Guitar* magazine, where I was a writer at the time. I spoke to his manager and said, "Look, does Glenn want to do a book?" And he said, "Yeah, funny enough, he does. He's looking for someone. So, it's good timing." Glenn's the best. He's a good friend of mine.

**Jon Sheasby:** I saw him in 2015 with Doug Aldrich on guitar and Pontus Engborg on drums, and I couldn't believe how good they were.

**Joel McIver:** He's amazing. He's great in any scenario, Glenn. I love him. Sitting down with him and hearing those old stories as well. That's nuts! [Laughs.] He should just do a spoken word tour. In fact, I might suggest that he go and meet people and tell stories because he has lived through some mental things.

**Jon Sheasby:** So, which autobiographies have been your favorite to work on so far?

**Joel McIver:** They're all good fun. I did one with Thunder [*Thunder: Giving the Game Away: The Official Biography*] a few years ago, and that was a blast because they're all geezers, and they take the piss, and they've got a really funny sense of humor. I went and traveled around with them to their childhood homes and spent time with those guys and really got to know them. They're brilliant. There are no pretensions about them. Max's book was obviously a high point. They're all really good to do.

Joel McIver at book signing
Courtesy of Joel McIver

There hasn't been one that hasn't been an absolute laugh. The one with Glen Matlock [*Glen Matlock's Sex Pistols Filthy Lucre Photo File*] was a lot of fun. I did Cannibal Corpse's official book [*Bible of Butchery: Cannibal Corpse, The Official Biography*], which was brilliant because those guys are just really sweet. The one I did with this Icelandic band, Skálmöld [*The Saga of Skálmöld*], was wicked because I went up to Reykjavík and spent some time with them while they were recording an album. And then I got the president of Iceland [Guðni Th. Jóhannesson] to do the foreword, which is mental.

**Jon Sheasby:** [Laughs.]

**Joel McIver:** The one I did with Frank Bello of Anthrax [*Fathers, Brothers, and Sons: Surviving Anguish, Abandonment, and Anthrax*] was really, really good. They're all great. It's always a privilege to do it. And the one I did with Right Said Fred [*Still Too Sexy: Surviving Right Said Fred*] a few years ago was funny. We went and spent a week away in a cottage in Devon and just filled the house with beer, let the recorder roll, and did it all in one go.

**Jon Sheasby:** How did that book come about?

**Joel McIver:** I'd been friends with Fred Fairbrass on Facebook for a while and dropped him a line. And we ended up meeting and talking about a book. Then we got a deal with Omnibus Press and went and did it. It was an absolute laugh. It was brilliant.

**Jon Sheasby:** Yeah, because comparing it to some of your other work is quite different.

**Joel McIver:** Just a bit, right?

**Jon Sheasby:** I think it's interesting that you're curious about working with different artists and conversing with various people from different genres to see things from their perspective rather than just writing about the heaviest of metal bands.

**Joel McIver:** Yeah. I mean, I've done so much of that. I did a book [*I Am Morbid: Ten Lessons Learned from Extreme Metal, Outlaw Country, and the Power of Self-Determination*] with David Vincent from Morbid Angel as well. I've just covered so much extreme, brutal, violent music over the years. And the people are really nice. In my experience, the heavier the music, the nicer the people. Because they let it all out onstage, right? They know what they're doing is theatrically ridiculous and funny and have a sense of humor about it. My view is that I would work with anyone who's interesting and decent. And all the people I've worked with are, and they have an interesting story to tell. But it doesn't have to be music. I write a lot about history, politics, film, etc. The world is populated by interesting people, and it's great to hear their stories.

**Jon Sheasby:** You've also worked for various newspapers and magazines, editing both *Bass Guitar* and *Bass Player* magazine. So how does that compare to writing your own books?

**Joel McIver:** Well, it's completely different because you don't have any autonomy. In the case of the magazines I edited, I did that for ten years for two or three different publishers. And it's great, but it's working in a team. So you've got to manage people. You've got to manage upwards as well. You've got to manage your management. And you're on a schedule which is not determined by you. So the job of writing and organizing stuff is basically the same thing, but it's different because you have other people to account for and people telling you what to do. I don't mind that if it's good people, and I think, generally, in the case of those magazines, the people were all really good to work with. But I think, all in all, I prefer just to do my own thing, doing a book with whoever it is. Sitting down with them, their manager, the publisher, and getting it done. There aren't so many people involved, and I can figure out my own timeline, control my hours at work and so on. That suits me more, but I'm happy to be in either situation as long as the people are decent, the job is good, and the conditions are good.

**Jon Sheasby:** As a bass player yourself, was being a working musician something you ever pursued?

**Joel McIver:** No, but I've been thinking lately I probably should have done. Because in the Britpop era, I was living really close to London. And I really should have started a band in London and pushed it, but I never did. I think I couldn't be bothered. [Laughs.] I've done gigs since I was a teenager, and the idea didn't really appeal to me. So I have occasionally thought about it, but not in any really serious way. Making a living and touring the world would definitely be fun for a few years. I don't regret it, but that would have been a nice thing to do. I've been on a few tour buses. I did a thing with Kreator a few years ago. I got on that bus. Obviously, I was on Cannibal Corpse's bus for quite a while, as well. Traveling up and down is quite good fun, but after a while, you get sick of not having access to decent food and showers and never getting any sleep. It's exhausting. But it's definitely fun to do the rock and roll thing for a little while. It's a great way to make a living and a bit of a surreal existence. And I think it's a pretty good way to avoid growing up. [Laughs.]

**Jon Sheasby:** I've just got one more question before we wrap up, Joel. So I just want to thank you for your input.

**Joel McIver:** No, not at all, mate. Thanks for getting in touch.

**Jon Sheasby:** I'd just like to ask you what your reaction was when an extinct species of brittle star [Ophiolofsson joelmciveri] was named after you by Professor Mats E. Eriksson and his colleagues at Lund University, Sweden? That has to be something that's far too surreal to comprehend, right?

**Joel McIver:** Dude, I was so happy. If you asked me if I wanted a knighthood or a species of brittle star named after me, I'd have taken the brittle star. [Laughs.] At fifty-three, I just had it tattooed on my arm too, and I've never had a tattoo. That's what it means to me, and I probably won't get another one. Yeah, it's huge for me. So the paleontologist Mats Eriksson, who discovered it and named it after me, is a fan of my Cannibal Corpse book. He got in touch a few years ago, and we became Facebook friends. He dropped me a line and said he really enjoyed the book, and he had also named a fossil after the bass player of Cannibal Corpse, Alex Webster, as well as other people. He got in touch and said he would do this one for me, which blew my mind. The short answer is that it absolutely fucking blew my mind. I'm so happy about that. It's a big deal.

**Jon Sheasby:** Yeah, it is. I can't even imagine it happening, so congrats on that!

**Joel McIver:** You never know. One day, make friends with a paleontologist. That's what I suggest! [Laughs.]

**Jon Sheasby:** [Laughs.] Well, cheers, Joel. I appreciate the conversation.

**Joel McIver:** And you. I hope we have a pint someday.

CHAPTER 10
# New Beginnings, New Millennium, New Status Quo

As 1999 drew to a close, there was no denying that a changing pop culture landscape was arriving. As with grunge's mainstream dominance at the start of the decade before, alternative music was once again thriving on the US *Billboard* 200 chart at the beginning of the new millennium. Bands like Disturbed and Linkin Park would avoid the pitfalls that led to nu-metal's downward spiral by evolving the style to even greater heights, shattering chart records and earning widespread acclaim in the process. My Chemical Romance, Fall Out Boy, and Paramore successfully merged pop-punk and emo, popularizing a subculture that defined a generation of introverted teens. And Canada's Nickelback mixed post-grunge with arena rock, becoming *Billboard*'s most successful rock group of the '00s.

Not only was alternative music once again flourishing in North America, but a surge of US-influenced acts also caught traction over on my side of the pond. UK bands like Busted and McFly, for instance, found much inspiration in the pop-punk activities of Blink-182, shaping a brand-new generation of groups like US teen idols the Jonas Brothers and Australian golden boys 5 Seconds of Summer. Welsh heavy metal band Bullet for My Valentine merged old-school thrash with nu-metal, melodic metalcore, and emo, landing three separate studio albums— 2008's *Scream Aim Fire*, 2010's *Fever*, and 2015's *Venom*—among the US

*Billboard* 200's top ten. (The band's 2005 debut, *The Poison*, was certified gold in the US on January 30, 2009.)

Surprisingly, even pop sensation Ed Sheeran's colossal triumphs on both sides of the Atlantic led to multiple collaborations with Eminem, the chance to hang out with Korn backstage at a Marilyn Manson show, and the opportunity to cover Limp Bizkit's "Break Stuff" during an appearance on *The Tonight Show Starring Jimmy Fallon*. MTV was also going through its own transitional phase during the 2000s, with more time dedicated to the noxious outbreak of reality TV and less to that which had first made MTV a household name: music. The success of *The Real World*, which launched in 1992 and is often cited as the show that began the modern reality TV plague, played a central role in the development of later "unscripted" hits like *Newlyweds: Nick and Jessica*, *Laguna Beach: The Real Orange County*, and *My Super Sweet 16*.

Additional commissions, such as the ghastly plastic-surgery-focused *I Want a Famous Face* and the cruelty-disguised-as-comedy dating series *Next*, furthered MTV's dominion over the reality TV space. Fortunately, not every show it produced during this period was as brain numbingly repellent. The animated sitcom *Daria*, a spinoff of Mike Judge's Gen X satire *Beavis and Butt-Head*, was met with much acclaim from its inception and consistently ranked among MTV's highest-rated shows during its 1997 to 2002 run. *Celebrity Deathmatch*, the adult Claymation parody series, similarly proved to be a hit before moving to MTV2 in 2006 for its fifth season. However, one distinct stunt comedy show—and its ragtag exhibitionist stars—stands on its own as a cultural touchstone for the MTV2 Generation.

Debuting on October 1, 2000, MTV's *Jackass* indulged in the delinquent stupidity of grown men, often featured Tony Hawk in a recurring capacity, and catered to the skate-punk crowd with music from the Bloodhound Gang and CKY, though like so many of this book's subjects, *Jackass* (and its numerous spinoffs, such as *Viva La Bam* and *Wildboyz*) didn't come without controversy. The show's cult popularity amidst young audiences became a cause of concern among politicians—including Joe Lieberman, a US Senator from Connecticut between 1989 and 2013—who urged MTV to take more accountability for promoting the encouragement of reckless behavior and do more to help parents safeguard their children from copying the show's stunts. (*Jackass* repeatedly featured disclaimers—before, during, and after the show—warning of the dangers of recreating the stunts.)

This kind of unwanted attention led to a disagreement between MTV and the *Jackass* crew about the show's future on the channel, ultimately resulting in its transition to the big screen, where its creators could circumvent the chance of kids stumbling across the stunts on TV and were better protected against any lawsuits due to the film's restricted admittance among those without adult supervision. I can honestly say I got nothing out of *Jackass* other than pure, unadulterated laughs. Long

*Jackass Forever* movie poster
Courtesy of Paramount Pictures

before my default setting became a jaded cynic upon turning on the news every morning, at no point did I ever think watching Johnny Knoxville wearing firework-propelled roller skates looked like a good idea, nor do I believe *Jackass* gets enough credit for being as subversive as it truly was.

I grew up watching *Jackass* and its spinoffs, so it should go without saying that I have a particular fondness for its cast and the years of laughs they gave me. This might sound crass to those who've never seen a second of the franchise, but at a time in which the entertainment industry was systemically failing women via hypersexualization, the titular jackasses were more than happy to put their genitalia in excruciatingly painful situations for the amusement of others. This ball-breaking, taboo-busting obsession with putting one's manhood in all sorts of precarious predicaments stood in contrast to the era's hierarchical gender conventions, squashing the macho customs being promoted elsewhere, and complemented the film antics of *American Pie* and music by Blink-182.

But as much as I've loved watching the gang over the years, I do hope they'll give themselves a well-earned rest after reuniting in 2022 for their fifth big-screen outing, *Jackass Forever*, which feels like both the perfect sendoff for the original crew and a sidesplitting introduction to a new bunch of numskulls (and a girl!) who are more than capable of continuing *Jackass*'s legacy for years to come. (Thus far, *Jackass* has expanded to five theatrically released feature films and earned close to $600 million at the worldwide box office. The franchise's fourth installment, *Jackass Presents: Bad Grandpa*, was even honored with an Academy Award nomination— losing to *Dallas Buyers Club* for Best Makeup and Hairstyling—at the 86th Academy Awards on March 2, 2014.)

Which brings me back to the music that inspired this book in the first place. Obviously, I've written extensively about the year 1999 and the likes of Eminem, Marilyn Manson, Blink-182, Limp Bizkit, and Creed—but they're just a few of the many who influenced the alternative music scene of my childhood. Whom would you choose if you had to pick fifty essential artists who defined the MTV2 Generation? Just fifty artists out of hundreds—if not thousands—of alternative, hip-hop, nu-metal, pop-punk, and post-grunge acts that soundtracked the lives of millions of teens worldwide. Artists who took up every space—of the thirty available, if the files were small enough—on my first-ever 128MB MP3 player. (Kids today don't know how lucky they are to have so much music readily available in the palm of their hands!)

An unenviable task, sure, but not one without the enjoyment of spending time listening to all the artists who first inspired me as a kid, helped me through my most difficult periods, and continue to be featured on random Spotify playlists all these years later. It's sad, then, that in doing so I came to realize just how many of those performers have passed away. Some, tragically, died by suicide. Others lost their battle with chemical dependencies. A few were also unfortunate to succumb to natural causes. But what all of them have in common is that they were far too young to leave this mortal plane, which makes me appreciate all the more their music, their gift of sharing it with us, and the immortal power of art.

The only restriction I placed on myself in narrowing the list to fifty entries is that none of the artists could've released their debut studio album before 1990, which is why some perennial favorites of MTV2 Generation—such as the Red Hot Chili Peppers, Nine Inch Nails, and the Offspring—fail to make an appearance. With all that in mind, I think we're just about ready to dust off that Sony Walkman, fire up that dial-up modem, and remember a more innocent time in life with this alphabetical look back at my picks for the fifty essential artists who defined the MTV2 Generation . . .

*CHAPTER 11*
# 50 Essential Artists Who Defined the MTV2 Generation

**1. Alien Ant Farm**

Only a handful of artists are brave enough to cover some of music's all-time greats. Some would say it's stupid even to attempt to improve on perfection. So who back in 2001 could've foreseen the sensation that was Alien Ant Farm's Grammy-nominated cover of Michael Jackson's "Smooth Criminal," which not only hit number one on the US *Billboard* Modern Rock Tracks chart but also spent an astonishing eight weeks atop Australia's ARIA Singles Chart, the joint first longest-running number-one single of the year (alongside "Angel" by Jamaican reggae artist Shaggy). The success of "Smooth Criminal," later featured in *American Pie 2* and released as the second single from the band's platinum-selling second studio album, *Anthology*, saw Alien Ant Farm soar to the peak of its career.

The accompanying music video to "Smooth Criminal" even got the approval of the song's creator, who gave the thumbs up after his request to reshoot a few scenes was granted. *Anthology*'s first single, "Movies," was later rereleased after the success of "Smooth Criminal" and became a hit in its own right, reaching number five in the UK, forty-eight places higher than its original peak position of fifty-three. While Alien Ant Farm would thereafter struggle to match the heights of its early success, the band remains one of the key figures from the late 1990s/early 2000s alternative scene and will be remembered for bringing a sense of humor to the hostile aggression for which nu-metal is better known. Alien Ant Farm released its sixth and most recent studio album, *Mantras*, in 2024.

## 2. The All-American Rejects

Achieving fame from the get-go with its 2002 self-titled debut studio album, the All-American Rejects can count itself as one of the most successful punk-adjacent bands to have thrived in the wake of Blink-182's *Enema of the State*. Fronted by musician-turned-actor Tyson Ritter, the band hit the ground running with the success of its first single, "Swing, Swing," which peaked at number eight on the US *Billboard* Modern Rock Tracks chart in March 2003. The band's 2005 second studio album, *Move Along*, became an even bigger hit, generating three top fifteen US *Billboard* Hot 100 singles, which not only helped propel the album to number six on the US *Billboard* 200 but also saw it eventually reach three-times-platinum status in December 2024.

The band's 2008 third studio album, *When the World Comes Down*, saw its biggest commercial success to date thanks to the album's lead single, "Gives You Hell," which topped both the US *Billboard* Mainstream Top 40 and Adult Top 40 charts, peaked at number four on the US *Billboard* Hot 100, and later went on to be certified nine-times-platinum after shipping nine million copies in the US alone. A reported twelve million album sales, multiple platinum certifications, and a Best Group Video win at the 2006 MTV Video Music Awards saw the Stillwater, Oklahoma, natives flourish during the 2000s second wave of pop-punk. The band's achievements were also recognized by its home state when the All-American Rejects were honored with the 2008 Rising Star award by the Oklahoma Music Hall of Fame.

## 3. Atreyu

Atreyu was named after the character Atreyu from German author Michael Ende's 1979 fantasy novel, *The Neverending Story*, later adapted into Wolfgang Petersen's much-loved 1984 adventure film of the same name, and you'd be forgiven for thinking a band that would purposefully name itself after the young warrior was as soft as his friendly dragon companion, Falkor. However, the band's music draws from many influences, often combining—especially in the early years—the blunt force riffing of metal, the lyrically emotional themes of screamo, and the all-black-clothed/finger-polished fashion stylings of goth. (YouTube Atreyu's video for "Lip Gloss and Black," the second single from its 2002 debut studio album, *Suicide Notes and Butterfly Kisses*, to see what I mean!)

As Atreyu prepared for its next studio album, 2004's gold-certified *The Curse*, the "Lip Gloss and Black" video gave the band an early flirtation with the mainstream after receiving extensive airplay on MTV2's revitalized *Headbangers Ball*. That album's success earned Atreyu greater exposure and a spot on 2005's *Mr. & Mrs. Smith* soundtrack, which features its cover of the Bon Jovi classic "You Give Love a Bad Name," bolstering the career-high chart performances of the band's following two studio albums, 2006's *A Death-Grip on Yesterday* and 2007's *Lead Sails Paper Anchor*, which peaked at number nine and eight on the US *Billboard* 200 respectively. Atreyu, now fronted by former drummer Brandon Saller, released its latest studio album, *The Beautiful Dark of Life*, in 2023.

## 4. Avenged Sevenfold

I don't think it would be an exaggeration to say that no other band/artist on this list has gone through a more considerable evolution—both creatively and personally—than Grammy nominee Avenged Sevenfold. While the band's first two studio albums, 2001's *Sounding the Seventh Trumpet* (a rushed, cheaply produced debut) and 2003's *Waking the Fallen* (a substantially better, more refined effort), have their fair share of fans who would argue a preference for both records' rawness, it was 2005's triumphant *City of Evil* that fully captured Avenged Sevenfold's unique sound for the first time. (The album's second single, "Bat Country," reached number one on *TRL*'s daily music video countdown and helped the band win the 2006 MTV Video Music Award for Best New Artist in a Video.)

Landing somewhere among the harmonious twin-guitar sound of Judas Priest, the attitude of Guns N' Roses, and the macabre theatricality of a Tim Burton-directed/Danny Elfman-composed film, Avenged

Sevenfold's idiosyncratic style has seen the band evolve into one of the most ambitiously creative and commercially successful acts of the past twenty-five years, having twice topped the US *Billboard* 200 chart. But things haven't always been plain sailing for the quintet, as the 2009 death of twenty-eight-year-old Jimmy "The Rev" Sullivan—the band's virtuoso drummer, pianist, covocalist, and cosongwriter—forced Avenged Sevenfold to consider its future. Ultimately, the band continued after Sullivan's passing, first with Mike Portnoy and then with Arin Ilejay, before settling with Brooks Wackerman in 2015.

### 5. Avril Lavigne

While female-fronted rock bands have enjoyed significant commercial success for decades, the 1990s gave way to a plethora of alternative acts like No Doubt and Hole, who are equally responsible for empowering a generation of young women and breaking down gender stereotypes with reckless abandon. One such successor, Avril Lavigne, became a phenomenon in the early 2000s, and I have such vivid memories of listening to her 2002 debut studio album, *Let Go*, particularly the album's first two singles, "Complicated" and "Sk8er Boi," which bookended my shift from ten-year-old primary schooler to eleven-year-old high schooler. (More than twenty years after its release, *Let Go* is still the best-selling album of the twenty-first century by a Canadian artist, with sales in excess of sixteen million units.)

And while Lavigne's success in the primarily male-dominated world of pop-punk is unrivaled, her legacy goes far beyond two number ones on the US *Billboard* 200, eight Grammy nominations, and one win from seven nominations at the MTV Video Music Awards, helping pave the way for Gen Z's more diverse and emotionally mature reinvention of pop-punk with the likes of Olivia Rodrigo. Now, more than twenty years after *Let Go* (and if her weekend-stealing performance at the 2024 Glastonbury Festival is anything to go by), I'd go as far as to say that Lavigne is about to enter the most interesting period of her career, having positioned herself first in line to take on the mantle currently held by Blondie's Debbie Harry in keeping the spirit of pop-punk young and relatable for many years to come.

## 6. Blink-182

Emerging from the fruitful Southern California skate-punk scene (which has similarly nurtured the Offspring, Green Day, and No Doubt), MTV Video Music Award winner Blink-182 positioned itself as the de facto leader of the second wave of pop-punk with the release of its third studio album, 1999's generation-defining *Enema of the State*. By accurately representing the hormonal awkwardness of teenage life, combined with its slick production values and impossibly catchy melodies, *Enema of the State* is unquestionably one of the most influential records of the past twenty-five years, having gone on to sell over fifteen million copies worldwide. (In 2017, *Kerrang!* named *Enema of the State* atop its list of "The 51 Greatest Pop-Punk Albums of All Time.")

While breakups, makeups, and personal grievances among the classic trio have seen the band's autobiographical lyrics materialize into existence like a real-life soap opera, the addition of guitarist/vocalist Matt Skiba—who replaced Tom DeLonge between 2015 and 2022—saw the new lineup's first record together, 2016's *California*, debut at number one on the US *Billboard* 200, the band's first time doing so since the 2001 release of its fourth studio album, *Take Off Your Pants and Jacket*. (*California* would also earn Blink-182 its first-ever Grammy nomination for Best Rock Album.) With the classic trio back together, 2023's *One More Time . . .* became the band's third chart-topping album on the US *Billboard* 200, proving plenty of life remains in these middle-aged dogs.

## 7. Bloodhound Gang

Despite never receiving particularly positive reviews from mainstream critics, the Bloodhound Gang has carved out a niche but loyal audience with its salacious lyrics and bawdy onstage escapades. Perhaps best known for the song "The Bad Touch," officially released in most territories as the second single from the band's third and most successful studio album, 1999's platinum-certified *Hooray for Boobies*, the Bloodhound Gang surprisingly found itself on the edge of the mainstream. Boosted by the song's success, especially in Europe, where it reached number one in several countries, *Hooray for Boobies* debuted on the US *Billboard* 200 at number nineteen in early 2000 before climbing to its peak of number fourteen just under a month later.

A favorite of Bam Margera, of MTV's *Jackass* and *Viva La Bam* fame, the band has never shied away from some of its more outrageous proclivities, having caused controversy on numerous occasions in multiple countries, typically thanks to the antics of bassist "Evil" Jared Hasselhoff (Jared Hennegan). Hasselhoff's tendency to publicly urinate at any given time has seen him fined $10,000 while filming *Viva La Bam* and shocking audiences at the 2006 editions of both the Rock am Ring and Pinkpop music festivals. A 2013 trip to Ukraine and Russia didn't go well either after the band was assaulted at the airport because of Hasselhoff's onstage profanities involving both countries' respective flags. The Bloodhound Gang's fifth and most recent studio album, *Hard-Off*, was released in 2015.

### 8. Bowling for Soup

Famed for its goofy sense of humor and comical music videos, Bowling for Soup stands alongside Blink-182 as one of the definitive second-wave pop-punk bands of the 2000s. Fronted by the zany charms of singer/guitarist Jaret Reddick, the band preludes Blink-182's recording career, debuting in 1994 with its self-titled first studio album, but struggled to find success—like so many of its contemporaries—until after the release of *Enema of the State*. Bowling for Soup's breakthrough record, 2002's fourth studio album, *Drunk Enough to Dance*, rejuvenated its career, spurred on by the band's Grammy-nominated hit single, "Girl All the Bad Guys Want," which peaked at number eight in the UK on August 17, 2002.

The band's subsequent two records, 2004's *A Hangover You Don't Deserve* and 2006's *The Great Burrito Extortion Case*, found similar success, yielding two of its most famous songs, "1985" and "High School Never Ends," respectively. While the band would never match the commercial heights of Blink-182, it has found longevity through endless appearances on film and TV soundtracks (including cameos in 2002's *Crossroads* and 2005's *Cursed*), as well as its association with Nickelodeon and the Disney Channel, the former of which hired Bowling for Soup to compose the theme song to the 2001 Academy Award-nominated film *Jimmy Neutron: Boy Genius*. (The band also performed the theme for the Disney Channel's animated musical-comedy show *Phineas and Ferb*.)

## 9. Crazy Town

Too hip-hop to be openly appreciated by the metal crowd and too metal to be championed by hip-hop fans, Crazy Town became the true definition of a one-hit wonder when the band burst onto the scene with its chart-topping US *Billboard* Hot 100 smash, "Butterfly," released in October 2000. Based on a looped sample of a hypnotic John Frusciante guitar lick from the Red Hot Chili Peppers' 1989 instrumental "Pretty Little Ditty," the song became one of the irrefutable crossover hits for the MTV2 Generation with its radio-friendly blend of hip-hop and rock. Complemented by its dream-like music video, "Butterfly" drove Crazy Town's debut studio album, *The Gift of Game*, to platinum status, selling more than 1.6 million units in the US alone.

A spot opening for the Red Hot Chili Peppers followed the album's release, as did a place on both the 2000 and 2001 Ozzfest tours, but the band struggled to win over the die-hard metal fanatics in attendance, who were less than enthused by its commercialized look and sound. Unfortunately, success for Crazy Town was limited thereafter. The band's 2002 follow-up, *Dark Horse*, peaked at number 120 on the US *Billboard* 200, and its latest full-length release, 2015's *The Brimstone Sluggers*, failed to chart at all. Crazy Town's 2024 EP, *Flirting with Disaster*, would be its last with cofounding front man Seth "Shifty Shellshock" Binzer, who sadly passed away from an accidental drug overdose at the age of forty-nine in June of the same year, leaving the band's future in doubt.

## 10. Creed

Despite being one of the most commercially successful rock bands to have emerged in the mid-to-late 1990s, Creed—the twice MTV Video Music Award-nominated, Grammy Award-winning post-grunge superstars—has never felt the same level of love from critics, who've spent decades relentlessly mocking the band's supposed lack of originality and diluted pseudo-grunge shallowness. Scott Stapp's biblically inspired lyrics and Eddie Vedder-like baritone vocal delivery also have their detractors, but it's the opinions of fans who buy the records that truly matter, and a reported fifty million worldwide album sales speak louder than topping the 2013 *Rolling Stone*-published readers' poll "The Ten Worst Bands of the Nineties" ever could.

Before the band's 2004 breakup, Creed's relatively short recording career didn't hinder its ability to sell records in the millions, amassing three consecutive multiplatinum albums—1997's *My Own Prison*, 1999's *Human Clay*, and 2001's *Weathered*—the last two of which peaked at number one on the US *Billboard* 200. (*Human Clay* remains one of the best-selling albums of all time and contains the band's highest charting single, "With Arms Wide Open," which topped the US *Billboard* Hot 100 in late 2000 and won the Grammy Award for Best Rock Song the following year.) Tensions within the band have resulted in only one record in the past fifteen years, 2009's fourth studio album, *Full Circle*, but Creed's second reunion, in 2023, has sparked a resurgence in popularity and hope for new music.

### 11. Deftones

One of the most influential alternative bands to emerge after grunge's demise, Deftones has built its career on a fluid and experimental approach to music making, rendering it nigh impossible to pin the band to a specific genre. More often associated with alternative metal, for lack of a better descriptor, the band's diverse influences—ranging from shoegaze and nu-metal to post-punk and stoner rock—has been met with critical acclaim throughout its career, earning Deftones the 2001 Grammy Award for Best Metal Performance for the track "Elite" from its third studio album, *White Pony*. (The band's ninth studio album, 2020's double-Grammy-nominated *Ohms*, was named the best album of the year by *Loudwire*, *Metal Hammer*, and *Revolver*.)

Unfortunately, like so many bands on this list, Deftones has similarly lived through its own tragedy with the 2013 death of Chi Cheng, the band's bassist between 1990 and 2008, whose serious injuries after a 2008 car crash left him semicomatose for the last five years of his life. The band's final album recorded with Cheng, the tentatively titled *Eros*, remains unfinished after work on the record was halted in favor of starting over with a new, more positive-sounding album, 2010's *Diamond Eyes*, the first to feature friend of the band Sergio Vega as Cheng's replacement. (*Eros* remains shelved indefinitely, and its existence has become a part of music folklore, taking on a near-mythical status among unreleased albums.)

## 12. Disturbed

An immediate success upon the release of its 2000 debut studio album, *The Sickness*, Disturbed can count itself as a giant among heavy metal's modern crop with a reported seventeen million worldwide record sales, five consecutive US number-one albums, and three Grammy nominations. Fronted by David Draiman, one of the most recognizable voices of the past twenty-five years, who's revered for combining heavily distorted operatic vocals with percussively obtuse ad-libs and best exemplified on one of Disturbed's most notable songs, "Down with the Sickness," the Chicago natives have stuck to their guns and ignored the ever-changing trends of rock music throughout the band's career. (In 2016, "Down with the Sickness" was named the "Best Metal Song of the 21st Century" by *Loudwire*.)

While *The Sickness*, in terms of sales, remains Disturbed's most successful album, with five-times-platinum status for shipments of over five million copies in the US alone, the band's five-album stretch of consecutive number-one debuts on the US *Billboard* 200 chart—2002's *Believe*, 2005's *Ten Thousand Fists*, 2008's *Indestructible*, 2010's *Asylum*, and 2015's *Immortalized*—has forever earned Disturbed a place in music history as only the third band to accomplish such a feat, after Metallica and Dave Matthews Band. As of 2025, the band's success shows no signs of slowing down after its 2015 cover of the Simon & Garfunkel classic "The Sound of Silence" became an unlikely viral hit on TikTok, reentering the charts in 2024 thanks to a remix by Australian DJ and record producer CYRIL.

## 13. Drowning Pool

Named after the Paul Newman-starring 1975 film, Drowning Pool is yet another band to have persevered in the face of heartbreak, in this case the 2002 death of original lead singer Dave Williams. Williams's death from heart failure at the age of just thirty occurred during the band's tour in support of its 2001 debut studio album, *Sinner*, which debuted at number fourteen on the US *Billboard* 200 in June of the same year. As the band's only studio album to feature Williams's vocals, *Sinner* remains its most successful release, earning Drowning Pool its only platinum-certified studio album. The band's controversial first single and most well-known song, "Bodies," which became its only platinum-certified single, was crucial to *Sinner*'s success.

The song, while heavily promoted and popularized by WWE and its ECW brand's extensive use between 2001 and 2008, became controversial due to its repeated use by the US military at the (still open) Guantanamo Bay detention camp. ("Bodies"'s notoriously misinterpreted lyrics, which the band asserts are about letting off steam and moshing during a live show, reportedly became a favorite of the interrogators at Guantanamo Bay between 2003 and 2006 and was used for ten days straight in the high-profile interrogation of Mohamedou Ould Salahi, the Mauritanian engineer notoriously imprisoned at the detention camp without charge from 2002 to 2016.) Drowning Pool followed *Sinner* with six more studio albums—featuring three different singers and released to varying success—before being rejoined in 2023 by Ryan McCombs of SOiL fame, who first fronted the band between 2005 and 2011.

## 14. Eminem

Among the best-selling music artists of all time, Eminem got off to a shaky start with the release of his 1996 debut studio album, *Infinite*, issued before he found his authentic voice under the guise of his Slim Shady alter ego. Once that persona had been unveiled, Eminem created a space for himself among hip-hop's elite, continuing the Beastie Boys' legacy of acceptance of white rappers in hip-hop by successfully navigating the murky waters of cultural appropriation. By leaning into the trailer-trash label that defined Eminem's early childhood, his transgressive work, starting with his 1999 second studio album, *The Slim Shady LP*, acted as a gateway that helped popularize hip-hop among the archetypal Middle American audience.

Eminem's success—as a solo artist and member of both D12 and Bad Meets Evil—has seen him amass a reported 220 million record sales, fifteen Grammy Awards, and fifteen MTV Video Music Awards, and he is the first artist in history to have ten albums consecutively debut atop the US *Billboard* 200 chart. His reach also extends beyond the music world as the song "Lose Yourself" from the soundtrack to *8 Mile*, the 2002 Eminem-starring film, won the 2003 Academy Award for Best Original Song, making him the first hip-hop artist to be honored with the category's golden statuette. Eminem's latest record, 2024's *The Death of Slim Shady (Coup de Grâce)*, gave him his fifteenth chart-topper—including collaborative, soundtrack, and compilation albums—on the US *Billboard* 200.

### 15. Evanescence

Led by the hauntingly beautiful voice of Amy Lee, one of the MTV2 Generation's most important female role models, Evanescence, blending symphonic goth rock and alternative metal grooves, developed into one of the most influential acts of the last twenty years. Evanescence debuted at a time when nu-metal was at its commercial peak, and the band's success sparked an increase in popularity in the US for fellow female-fronted goth-influenced bands Lacuna Coil, Nightwish, and Within Temptation, all of whom predate Evanescence and have enjoyed significant success across Europe for almost thirty years. (Evanescence's diamond-certified 2003 debut studio album, *Fallen*, is the sixth-best-selling record of the twenty-first century and remains the band's most successful, with over seventeen million sales worldwide.)

In addition to appearing on *Fallen*, "Bring Me to Life," Evanescence's debut single, was first released on the hit soundtrack to 2003's *Daredevil* and helped the band to two wins at the 2004 Grammy Awards, beating preceremony favorite 50 Cent to win Best New Artist. (The song also earned Evanescence two nominations—for Best New Artist in a Video and Best Rock Video—at the 2003 MTV Video Music Awards and topped the singles chart in both the UK and Australia.) While band members have come and gone since Evanescence's 1994 inception, Amy Lee remains the group's driving force, leading it to two consecutive number ones on the US *Billboard* 200 and inspiring a new generation of alternative metal acts like Poppy and Spiritbox.

### 16. Fall Out Boy

Fall Out Boy originates from the same Chicago hardcore scene from which bands like Hatebreed, Taking Back Sunday, and Rise Against were also founded, and its 2003 debut studio album, *Take This to Your Grave*, is often cited as being one of the underground touchstones that helped turn emo pop-punk into a major mainstream movement, triggering the formation of an abundance of beneficiaries like All Time Low and You Me at Six. The album's success also assisted with the setup of Decaydance Records, later renamed DCD2 Records, owned by bassist Pete Wentz. Fall Out Boy's 2005 second studio album, *From Under the Cork Tree*, enhanced the band's reputation further, debuting at number nine on the US *Billboard* 200 with first-week sales nearing 170,000 copies.

That album remains Fall Out Boy's most commercially successful, earning the band a Grammy nomination for Best New Artist, one win at both the 2005 and 2006 editions of the MTV Video Music Awards, and selling over seven million copies worldwide. Albums three and four, 2007's *Infinity on High* and 2008's *Folie à Deux*, were equally triumphant, with the former earning the band its first chart-topper on the US *Billboard* 200, but a hiatus between 2009 and 2013 left the quartet's future up in the air. Since reconciling, though, Fall Out Boy has released an additional four studio albums, the first three of which debuted atop the US *Billboard* 200 chart. The band also received its second Grammy nomination—for Best Rock Album—in 2019.

### 17. Foo Fighters

Initially started by Dave Grohl as a solo creative outlet while mourning the death of his Nirvana bandmate Kurt Cobain, Foo Fighters have crossed generations and outlived trends, earning a staggering fifteen Grammys, three MTV Video Music Awards, and two number ones on the US *Billboard* 200 and entered the Rock & Roll Hall of Fame in the band's first year of eligibility in 2021. Starting with *The Colour and the Shape*, the band's 1997 second studio album and first recorded with a complete lineup, Foo Fighters—then a four-piece—ushered in the post-grunge era with the album's three singles, "Monkey Wrench," "Everlong," and "My Hero," all of which have remained staples of the band's live show for almost thirty years and remain a mainstay on rock radio across the US.

As Foo Fighters approached the thirtieth anniversary of its formation, the band ventured into new territory with the February 25, 2022, release of its first nondocumentary feature film, *Studio 666*, a comedy-horror blend of *The Evil Dead* and *This Is Spinal Tap* helmed by *Hatchet III* director BJ McDonnell. While the film failed to ignite the box office in a world still recovering from the COVID-19 pandemic, the band would shortly thereafter be shaken by the sudden death of Taylor Hawkins, its longtime drummer and heroic everyman, on March 25, 2022. But despite Cobain's death spelling the end for Nirvana, Foo Fighters regrouped in 2023, a move celebrated by the sextet's fans and the music press alike, first with prolific session percussionist Josh Freese and then with former Nine Inch Nails drummer Ilan Rubin.

### 18. Fountains of Wayne

Cofounded by lead singer/rhythm guitarist Chris Collingwood and the band's late, great bassist and Academy Award-nominated songwriter, Adam Schlesinger, Fountains of Wayne appeared to be one of the few bands on this list to have ended for good, originally breaking up in 2013 after the tour for its fifth and final studio album, 2011's *Sky Full of Holes*. But the band almost didn't make it that far after a breakdown in communication between Atlantic Records and Fountains of Wayne led to the band being dropped by the label in 1999 after its first two albums failed to chart on the US *Billboard* 200. Thankfully, Fountains of Wayne's breakthrough came in 2003 with its most well-known song, "Stacy's Mom," the first single from the band's third studio album, *Welcome Interstate Managers*.

"Stacy's Mom"'s success revived the band's enthusiasm for creating music after a crushing period of inactivity followed its exit from Atlantic. (The song also earned the band two nominations at the 2004 Grammy Awards.) Although Schlesinger's death on April 1, 2020, seemingly signaled no hope for Fountains of Wayne's reconciliation, a one-off reunion on April 22, 2020—performed by the band's surviving members as part of a charity livestream event in tribute to its late bass player—led to a full reunion in 2025. (During his lifetime, Schlesinger's songwriting won three Emmys and one Grammy, and earned one nomination each at the Tony, Golden Globe, and Academy Awards, the last two of which for the song "That Thing You Do!" from the film of the same name.)

### 19. Good Charlotte

Good Charlotte is what happens when you mix equal parts of the Cure and Green Day—a pop-punk amalgamation of hair gel, mascara, and a wardrobe exclusively assembled from Hot Topic. After gaining some exposure opening for Blink-182 and Sum 41, the band perfected the sound of its self-titled debut studio album with its 2002 follow-up, *The Young and the Hopeless*, a bona fide pop-punk classic that ranks among the best from the era. The album's breakthrough was amplified by the success of the first single, "Lifestyles of the Rich and Famous," which took home the Viewer's Choice award at the 2003 MTV Video Music Awards and reached number eight in the UK in February of the same year.

The album's second and third singles, "The Anthem" and "Girls & Boys," were likewise hits in the UK, peaking at number ten and six respectively, pushing *The Young and the Hopeless* to three-times-platinum status in the US with sales of over three million copies by February 2004. The band returned in October 2004 with its third and highest-charting studio album yet, *The Chronicles of Life and Death*, which debuted at number three on the US *Billboard* 200 with first-week figures of 199,000 copies, earning the band the largest opening week sales of its career. Having had a stable five-piece lineup since 2005, the band continues to record and tour, releasing its eighth and most recent studio album, *Motel Du Cap*, in 2025.

## 20. Green Day

Out-and-out one of the key rock bands of the past thirty-five years, Green Day could've called it a day at the end of the 1990s, and it would still be recognized as one of the best punk bands of all time. From its 1990 debut studio album, *39/Smooth*, to 1997's fifth studio album, *Nimrod*, the band's catalogue of angst-ridden anthems revitalized punk rock for a new generation, directly leading to the second wave of pop-punk and the genre's explosion into the mainstream consciousness. (The band's first genuine classic, 1994's double-diamond-certified *Dookie*, won the 1995 Grammy Award for Best Alternative Album, has sold over twenty million copies in the US alone, and continues to garner critical acclaim thirty years after its original release.)

The band's evolution in the 2000s, especially in the writing and recording of its 2004 seventh studio album, *American Idiot*, inspired by the Who's 1969 rock opera, *Tommy*, further established Green Day's genius as songwriters, earning the band its first number-one album on the US *Billboard* 200 chart with 267,000 units sold in its first week. As of the 2024 release of its fourteenth studio album, *Saviors*, Green Day has sold approximately seventy-five million records worldwide, won five Grammys and twelve MTV Video Music Awards, debuted atop the US *Billboard* 200 with three separate albums, and entered the Rock & Roll Hall of Fame in its first year of eligibility, making the band one of the most successful acts in the history of music.

### 21. Hole

Nobody from the '90s alternative rock scene sparks as much debate and divisiveness as Hole's front woman, the irrepressible—and oft-time incoherent—Courtney Love. To many, she's a pioneer who stood apart from her flannel-wearing contemporaries with subversive individuality and a trailblazing rock star who proved that girls can rock—and party—just as hard as the boys. To others, she's somewhat of a conundrum and low-key figure in the death of her then husband, Kurt Cobain, the Nirvana icon and symbolic leader of Gen X. Nick Broomfield's 1998 documentary film, *Kurt & Courtney*, does much to negate any such complicity, but conspiracy theories surrounding Cobain's suicide will never cease to exist.

What isn't up for debate, however, is Hole's place among the pantheon of alternative '90s greats. A reported three million record sales, four Grammy nominations, and two MTV Video Music Award nominations make Hole one of the most commercially successful female-led alternative rock bands of all time, primarily due to its 1998 opus, *Celebrity Skin*. Spearheaded by Michael Beinhorn's production, the album's title track, "Celebrity Skin," which earned Hole its first and only number one on the US *Billboard* Modern Rock Tracks chart, assisted Hole in achieving one of the best-sounding albums of the decade. The crunchy guitar tones, rumbling bass, swinging drums, and Love's raspy vocal delivery gave *Celebrity Skin*'s pop-infused arrangements a glitzy sheen that would impress both mainstream critics and the alternative crowd alike.

### 22. Jimmy Eat World

Jimmy Eat World's sheer will to not give up and succeed in the face of failure, a model representation of the virtue of patience, is one of the main reasons why its success has created a feel-good factor and underdog spirit in the alternative community, who've championed the band's Rocky Balboa-like resilience for more than thirty years. Cited by bands like Dashboard Confessional and Paramore as a major influence, the emo kings struggled for ten years (taking on day jobs to offset the lack of commercial success) and produced three albums (none of which charted on the US *Billboard* 200) before the band's mainstream breakthrough came with its platinum-certified 2001 fourth studio album, *Bleed American*, which peaked at number thirty-one in the US.

After being dropped by Capitol Records following the release of its 1999 third studio album, *Clarity*, now considered among the best emo albums of all time, the band decided to self-finance its next record and chose to enter the studio as an unsigned act. The hype around *Bleed American*'s recording caused a bidding war among labels, with DreamWorks signing the band shortly before the album's release. All of the album's singles proved to be hits, but one, "The Middle," popularly regarded as Jimmy Eat World's signature song, became a worldwide sensation, peaking at number five on the US *Billboard* Hot 100 and topping the US *Billboard* Modern Rock Tracks chart in early 2002. (The song also earned the band its only MTV VMA nomination—for Best Rock Video—in 2002.)

### 23. Killswitch Engage

Hailing from the highly productive Massachusetts hardcore scene (responsible for the birth of All That Remains, Shadows Fall, and Unearth to name but a few), Killswitch Engage is often considered melodic metalcore's most influential band and the group that brought the genre into the mainstream in the early 2000s. Combining the more palatable elements of melodic death metal and metalcore, the band assisted extreme music's crossover to huge commercial success with its seminal 2002 second studio album, *Alive or Just Breathing*. While Killswitch Engage's original vocalist, Jesse Leach, quit shortly after the album's release (later returning to the fold in 2012), his replacement, Howard Jones, helped the band reach new heights.

Killswitch Engage's first two of three albums recorded with Jones,

2004's *The End of Heartache* and 2006's *As Daylight Dies*, peaked at number twenty-one and thirty-two on the US *Billboard* 200 respectively, later earning gold and platinum certifications from the RIAA. *The End of Heartache*'s title track, as well as "My Curse" and a cover of the Dio classic "Holy Diver" from *As Daylight Dies*, also performed well on singles charts, likewise earning gold and platinum certifications, with the former getting a Grammy nomination for Best Metal Performance in 2005. Since Leach's return in 2012, the band has amassed two additional Grammy nominations (both for Best Metal Performance) and reached a new peak of number six on the US *Billboard* 200 with the 2016 release of its seventh studio album, *Incarnate*.

### 24. Korn

While its members often distance themselves from the nu-metal tag, Korn is unquestionably one of the pioneers of alternative music's most divisive subgenre in terms of both its musical output and hip-hop-inspired dress code. The band's 1994 self-titled debut studio album (heavily inspired by the music of Faith No More, particularly Mike Patton's unconventionally singular vocals) influenced a generation of future acts—like Coal Chamber, Limp Bizkit, and Slipknot—with its innovative sound, which traded complex arrangements and guitar solos for syncopated hip-hop grooves and down-tuned riffing. Nu-metal's commercial growth can also be attributed to Korn's exposure on MTV, especially *TRL*, which gave significant airtime to the band's videos.

In fact, four of Korn's videos had to be retired from the show to allow more artists a chance at topping the daily video countdown, a fact that's all the more impressive given the band was battling for airtime against NSYNC and Britney Spears. Having recently celebrated the thirtieth anniversary of its debut studio album, the band can look back on its accomplishments with pride, having sold over forty million records worldwide, earning two number ones on the US *Billboard* 200, two wins from eight nominations at the Grammy Awards, and two MTV Video Music Awards in 1999 for its legendary video to one of the most popular songs of the MTV2 Generation, "Freak on a Leash." (In 2020, *Korn* placed first on *Kerrang!*'s list of "The 21 Greatest Nu-Metal Albums of All Time.")

## 25. Lamb of God

Formed in 1994 as Burn the Priest, the same name under which the band released its hardcore-punk-inspired 1999 debut studio album, five-time Grammy Award nominee Lamb of God is often considered among the leaders of the new wave of American heavy metal, having released some of the most acclaimed albums since the movement's formation. Starting with its ferocious second studio album and first under the Lamb of God name, 2000's *New American Gospel*, the Richmond, Virginia, natives lent into the groove metal sound that saw Pantera's 1994 seventh studio album, *Far Beyond Driven*, become the first extreme metal record to top the US *Billboard* 200. (Lamb of God's highest charting record came with the number two debut of its 2009 sixth studio album, *Wrath*.)

Lamb of God has continued to garner noteworthy success in the years since, but the 2012 arrest of the band's front man, Randy Blythe, charged with causing the death of a fan at a show in Prague, Czech Republic, two years earlier, was met with significant press coverage in the world of heavy metal. The verdict, rendered in 2013, held that Blythe was morally responsible for the fan's death, though not criminally liable. (The decision was upheld after an appeal against Blythe's acquittal was unsuccessful.) The 2014 documentary film *As the Palaces Burn*, titled after the band's 2003 third studio album of the same name, focuses on the events of Blythe's arrest, receiving generally favorable reviews upon release.

## 26. Limp Bizkit

Much to the chagrin of both critics and musically similar bands that preceded its formation, Limp Bizkit took the template established by Korn and turned it up to eleven, quickly becoming the nu-metal band against which all nu-metal bands are compared. Known for its rambunctious live shows and profanity-laden lyrics and Fred Durst's abrasive penchant for feuding with every major artist in the business, Limp Bizkit received mainstream attention from the outset, especially on *TRL*, which featured the band's Durst-directed music video for its cover of George Michael's "Faith" on heavy rotation. (Despite its success, the band placed third on *Rolling Stone*'s 2013 readers' poll "The Ten Worst Bands of the Nineties.")

Though the band's 1997 debut studio album, *Three Dollar Bill, Y'all*, earned Limp Bizkit a feverish cult following and platinum status by the decade's end, its subsequent two studio albums—1999's *Significant Other* and 2000's *Chocolate Starfish and the Hot Dog Flavored Water*—sent it into the stratosphere, netting the band three Grammy nominations, two consecutive number ones on the US *Billboard* 200, two MTV Video Music Awards, and over forty million record sales worldwide. Sadly, the band's performance in Leeds, England, on August 24, 2025, was its last with founding bassist Sam Rivers, who died on October 18, 2025, at the age of forty-eight. Limp Bizkit's sixth and most recent studio album, *Still Sucks*, was released in 2021.

## 27. Linkin Park

When Linkin Park's first studio album, 2000's *Hybrid Theory*, became the best-selling debut since Guns N' Roses's 1987 masterpiece, *Appetite for Destruction*, it was hard to imagine where they'd go from there. However, the band not only rose to the challenge but surpassed all expectations, becoming one of music's top-selling artists of all time, with estimated worldwide sales far exceeding one hundred million records. Linkin Park's electronica-heavy brand of lyrically intense but positively hopeful nu-metal immediately set it apart from the crowd, as did the back-and-forth between the group's colead vocalists, singer Chester Bennington and rapper Mike Shinoda, whose individual voices perfectly complemented the band's unique sound, helping create one of the most pivotal acts to have emerged at the start of the 2000s.

Since its 2000 debut, the band has won four MTV Video Music Awards and multiple Grammys, including the 2006 Grammy Award for Best Rap/Sung Collaboration (for "Numb/Encore") with Jay-Z. Linkin Park's philanthropic efforts haven't gone unnoticed either, as the band has gone above and beyond in the wake of natural disasters by raising millions in charitable donations during times of crisis. While Linkin Park's future remained in limbo after the 2017 suicide of Bennington, its 2024 comeback album with new singer Emily Armstrong, aptly titled *From Zero*, debuted at number two on the US *Billboard* 200 and reenergized the band's sound for a new generation. (In 2023, *Hybrid Theory* placed atop *Metal Hammer*'s list of "The 50 Best Metal Albums of the 2000s.")

## 28. Machine Head

Grammy nominee Machine Head, my personal favorite band to have debuted in my lifetime, were the first headline act sixteen-year-old me went to see live at the NEC Arena on Friday, November 23, 2007. The show—with supporting acts Trivium, DragonForce, Arch Enemy, and Shadows Fall—still stands as one of the best I've ever seen and set quite the benchmark for all future gigs. From the band's classic 1994 groove metal debut, *Burn My Eyes*, all the way through to its ripping eleventh record, 2025's *Unatoned*, Machine Head has never been afraid to experiment with its sound, often alienating its fan base with a style that's shifted from groove metal to nu-metal to thrash metal and beyond.

While membership has been somewhat of a revolving door, front man Robb Flynn has remained at the helm of Machine Head for more than thirty years, directing the band's evolution through thick and thin—including the fact the band's career was nearly ruined with the unfortunately timed music video for "Crashing Around You," released just before 9/11 and banned by MTV as a result of its imagery. In 2007, Machine Head released its sixth studio album, *The Blackening*, creating a modern metal masterwork and arguably the best heavy record of the twenty-first century so far. (Don't take just my word for it, though; it won Best Album at the 2007 *Kerrang!* Awards, was named *Metal Hammer*'s "Album of the Decade" in 2010 and was voted Roadrunner Records's "Album of the Century" in a 2011 poll.)

## 29. Marilyn Manson

Marilyn Manson's shock rock legacy has been somewhat tainted over the last few years by the assault allegations that have been leveled at not only the band's namesake lead singer but also former bassist Twiggy Ramirez. Not that controversy hasn't followed the band around since its inception, mind you, but firsthand accounts of abuse should always be treated far more seriously than any scandalous headline concocted by the news media. With that in mind and in no way downplaying the accusations, Marilyn Manson's contribution to the history of the MTV2 Generation shouldn't go unnoticed, particularly its revolutionary music videos, for which the band has won one MTV Video Music Award—for Best Cinematography in a Video—from five nominations.

While the band will be best remembered for its obscene music and knowingly shocking behavior, its condemnation of the news media's hypocritical glorification of real-life violence—stemming from infamously false allegations of influencing the culprits of the Columbine High School massacre—will go down in history as one of the turning points in '90s pop culture. The band continues to rewrite the story of its notorious legacy, having sold over fifty million records and accruing four Grammy nominations and two number ones on the US *Billboard* 200, and is now back out on the road in support of its twelfth studio album, 2024's *One Assassination Under God—Chapter 1*.

### 30. Mastodon

Sharing just as much in common—both musically and visually—with the prog rock artistry of King Crimson and Yes as it does with the abrasive heaviness for which metal is more commonly known, Mastodon more than lives up to the vision of the long-gone elephantine creature after which the band is named with a discography that's as celebrated as it is daunting. Through eight studio records and an assortment of compilations and EPs, the band has perfected the art of the prog metal concept album by blending densely imaginative lyrics, classically elemental themes, and ambitiously complex musicianship in an effort to distinguish itself from its peers and showcase its appreciation for myriad musical genres.

Until the 2025 departure of lead guitarist/covocalist Brent Hinds, who died in a motorcycle crash a few months later on August 20, 2025, the band had remained a steady four-piece lineup for over twenty years, finding critical acclaim from the outset with its 2002 debut studio album, *Remission*. (*Kerrang!* named *Remission* alongside albums like Eyehategod's *Take as Needed for Pain* and Crowbar's *Odd Fellows Rest* on its 2020 list of "The 13 Most Essential Sludge Records.") Mastodon scored its first Grammy nomination—for Best Metal Performance—in 2007 for "Colony of Birchmen," the third single from its 2006 third studio album, *Blood Mountain*, and has since gone on to win one award from six nominations in total, picking up the Best Metal Performance award in 2018 for the song "Sultan's Curse" from its seventh record, 2017's *Emperor of Sand*.

### 31. My Chemical Romance

From the band's inauspiciously raw 2002 debut studio album, *I Brought You My Bullets, You Brought Me Your Love*, to its 2010 pop rock opera curtain call, *Danger Days: The True Lives of the Fabulous Killjoys*, My Chemical Romance took the music world by storm, becoming emo pop-punk's breakout superstar during the scene's mainstream dominance. (I must admit, even I surrendered to the sway of the subculture's all-pervading presence during the 2000s, having dressed exclusively like an extra from one of the band's music videos during my midteens.) But while I have broadened my horizons beyond band T-shirts and have happily traded in Converse All Stars for more comfortable footwear, hearing My Chemical Romance's music still reminds me of the heightened emotions that came with being a teen.

And while I can understand My Chemical Romance wanting to distance itself from the emo tag, especially here in the UK, where the scene triggered unwarranted backlash from the press, including blatant falsities spread by the misinformed right-leaning tabloid, *The Daily Mail*, the band's importance to the '00s alternative music scene is beyond comparison. Since My Chemical Romance's inception, the band has been nominated for five MTV Video Music Awards and one Grammy, selling close to nine million albums in the US alone, and topping the UK singles chart with "Welcome to the Black Parade," the lead single from its 2006 third studio album, *The Black Parade*. (In 2021, *The Black Parade* placed first on *Kerrang!*'s list of "The 25 Greatest Emo Albums Ever.")

### 32. New Found Glory

Noted for its earnest lyrics and endless ability to write some of pop-punk's most memorable hooks, MTV Video Music Award nominee New Found Glory introduced itself to the world with the release of its debut studio album, *Nothing Gold Can Stay*, issued exactly one month before Blink-182's *Enema of the State*, on May 1, 1999. Perhaps setting the stage for the future success of the genre, the band's debut—the first of more than one dozen studio records—showcased its varied influences and helped create the blueprint for the future of pop-punk. While that album gave New Found Glory a platform from which to build, it took them only a little over a year to truly establish itself as one of pop-punk's leading voices with the 2000 release of its second studio album.

The band's major-label debut, *New Found Glory*, which reached number one on the US *Billboard* Heatseekers Albums chart, is often acclaimed as one of the genre's formative records by critics and musicians alike, going on to become the band's first gold-certified album. Its follow-up, 2002's *Sticks and Stones*, continued the band's upward trajectory, becoming its best-selling studio album (certified platinum in July 2020 for accumulating over one million sales) and first to enter both the US *Billboard* 200 and UK's top ten, peaking at number four in the US and number ten in the UK. New Found Glory earned its career-high peak of number three on the US *Billboard* 200 with the 2004 release of its fourth studio album, *Catalyst*.

### 33. Nickelback

The press would love you to believe that Nickelback, ranking behind only Creed on *Rolling Stone*'s 2013 poll "The Ten Worst Bands of the Nineties," is one of the worst bands of all time. However, Canada's finest have always dealt with the hate with a sense of humor, ignoring criticism by persevering with the style that placed the band behind only the Beatles among best-selling foreign acts on the US *Billboard* charts in the 2000s. (The band's breakthrough hit, "How You Remind Me," released as the lead single from its giant 2001 third studio album, *Silver Side Up*, topped the US *Billboard* Hot 100 and was played over 1.2 million times on US radio in the '00s, becoming the most requested song of the decade, according to Nielsen SoundScan.)

The band continues to sell out arenas worldwide with as much ease as it did at its peak, releasing a tribute to its fans with the 2023 documentary film *Hate to Love: Nickelback*, an intimate and celebratory look into the career of the 2023 Canadian Music Hall of Fame inductee, who've collected six Grammy nominations, won two MTV Video Music Awards, topped the US *Billboard* 200, and sold over fifty million records worldwide. (The band's fifth and most successful studio album, 2005's *All the Right Reasons*, was its first—and thus far only—to top the US

*Billboard* 200, earning diamond certification on March 3, 2017, for sales exceeding ten million units.)

### 34. No Doubt

No Doubt, one of the leaders of the third-wave ska revival alongside bands like Sublime and Less Than Jake, immediately set itself apart from the grunge sound that dominated the early '90s airwaves with its 1992 self-titled debut studio album. The band's success, however, was initially hampered by its record label's refusal to fund or promote the band's music appropriately. While this ultimately led No Doubt to finance and independently release its 1995 second studio album, *The Beacon Street Collection*, Interscope Records—with whom the band was still signed—agreed to bankroll its third record. Released just seven months after album number two, *Tragic Kingdom* became one of the decade's biggest hits, eventually reaching number one on the US *Billboard* 200 in December 1996.

The diamond-certified *Tragic Kingdom* not only turned No Doubt's singer, Gwen Stefani, into a global icon and won the band huge commercial success, spending nine nonconsecutive weeks atop the US *Billboard* 200 chart, but also saw the group receive approval from the Grammys (from whom it has won two awards from nine nominations) and mainstream attention from MTV (from whom it has won five Video Music Awards from eleven nominations). Included in those awards is a Best Group Video win for *Tragic Kingdom*'s monstrously popular third single, "Don't Speak," which spent sixteen weeks atop the US *Billboard* Hot 100 Airplay chart, peaked at number one in the UK, and has helped the band to over thirty million record sales worldwide.

### 35. OPM

Though not directly associated with the skate-punk movement that broke into the mainstream at the turn of the millennium, Los Angeles-based OPM benefited from the MTV2 Generation's obsession with *Tony Hawk's* video game series, becoming a one-hit wonder with its debut single, "Heaven Is a Halfpipe," released on June 27, 2000, as the lead single from the band's debut studio album, *Menace to Sobriety*. The song found moderate success in the US, reaching number eighteen on the

US *Billboard* Modern Rock Tracks chart, but was a bigger hit overseas, specifically in the UK, where it peaked at number four on July 14, 2001, debuting one place below Wheatus's cover of Erasure's synth-pop classic, "A Little Respect."

Whereas the album's second single, "El Capitan," also performed well in the UK, reaching the top twenty in January 2002, the band would struggle thereafter to replicate the success of "Heaven Is a Halfpipe," which took home the 2001 *Kerrang!* Award for Best Single, beating songs from such contemporary heavyweights as Limp Bizkit, Papa Roach, and Weezer. ("Heaven Is a Halfpipe" earned a gold certification in the UK on April 27, 2018, for sales surpassing 400,000 copies.) Unfortunately, the current status of OPM remains up in the air, as the band has not released a full-length studio album since its 2008 fourth record, *Golden State of Mind* (though it did release its fourth EP, *The Minge Dynasty*, in 2015).

## 36. P.O.D.

When you think of religious imagery in hard rock and heavy metal, you're more often than not met with themes of satanism, antireligion, and the iconic symbol of the Devil horns hand gesture. On the other side of the spectrum, a band like Stryper wore its Christian values on its sleeves and was able to build a sizable enough fan base for its 1986 third studio album, *To Hell with the Devil*, to become the first platinum-selling Christian metal record in the US. In the mid-1990s/early 2000s, a new wave of bands like Underoath and As I Lay Dying found comparable success within the world of metalcore, but nu-metal's P.O.D. transcended the religious crowd to become one of the genre's best-selling acts with the release of its three-times-platinum 2001 fourth studio album, *Satellite*.

Debuting at a career-high number six on the US *Billboard* 200 chart with first-week sales surpassing 133,000 copies, *Satellite* remains the band's most commercially successful and critically acclaimed album, having earned three Grammy nominations and six MTV Video Music Award nominations and accounts for over seven million of its combined total of twelve million record sales. Not only was the album a game changer for the band, but each of *Satellite*'s four singles—"Alive," "Youth of the Nation," "Boom," and "Satellite"—proved to be hits, especially the second of the four, which reached number one on the US *Billboard*

Modern Rock Tracks chart on March 30, 2002. The band's eleventh and most recent studio album, *Veritas*, was released in 2024.

### 37. Panic! at the Disco

Long before the name Panic! at the Disco became the moniker under which front man Brendon Urie performed (between 2015 and 2023) as a solo artist, the initial incarnation of the band attained fame as one of emo pop-punk's leading figures in the mid-2000s, finding immediate success upon the release of its 2005 debut studio album, *A Fever You Can't Sweat Out*. The record, released just under one year after the band's demo impressed Fall Out Boy's Pete Wentz, who subsequently signed the band to his newly created Decaydance Records in late 2004, was propelled up the charts by the success of *A Fever You Can't Sweat Out*'s second single, "I Write Sins Not Tragedies," which peaked at number seven on the US *Billboard* Hot 100, has been certified diamond in the US, and won the 2006 MTV Video Music Award for Video of the Year.

The band's following three albums—2008's *Pretty. Odd.*, 2011's *Vices & Virtues*, and 2013's *Too Weird to Live, Too Rare to Die!*—also proved to be extraordinarily successful, but Panic! at the Disco arguably hit its commercial peak once the group had disbanded and Urie decided to continue under the name as a solo performer. Urie's first album as a solo artist and fifth officially under the Panic! at the Disco name, 2016's *Death of a Bachelor*, became his first of two chart-toppers on the US *Billboard* 200, earning a nomination for Best Rock Album at the 2017 Grammy Awards. Panic! at the Disco's seventh and final studio album, *Viva Las Vengeance*, was released in 2022.

### 38. Papa Roach

While its self-funded 1997 debut studio album, *Old Friends from Young Years*, remains an elusive entry in the band's canon, Papa Roach rode the wave of nu-metal's breakthrough with its second record and major-label debut, 2000's *Infest*, which shot the band to fame in the early 2000s. The album's success, riding on the wings of its chart-topping US *Billboard* Modern Rock Tracks hit single, "Last Resort," eventually pushed *Infest* to peak at number five on the US *Billboard* 200 after it originally debuted at number forty-eight. The album's success also helped Papa Roach on its way to a Best New Artist in a Video nomination at the 2000 MTV Video Music Awards and two nominations at the 2001 Grammy Awards and has been certified four-times-platinum in the US.

What's more is that while Papa Roach's sound has shifted dramatically over the years, crossing from nu-metal to glam and even a flirtation with electronica with its 2012 seventh studio album, *The Connection*, the band has always been proud to have been a part of the nu-metal revolution despite some of its peers' disdain for their part in the scene's history. This humility is perhaps why Papa Roach has been able to achieve such permanency, as exemplified by the success of its eleventh studio album, 2022's *Ego Trip*, which produced the band's seventh, eighth, ninth, and tenth number ones on the US *Billboard* Mainstream Rock chart. (As of 2025, Papa Roach has earned an additional two number ones on the chart, tying the band for sixth overall on the chart's list of acts with the most chart-topping songs.)

### 39. Paramore

Appearing around the same time as fellow emo pop-punk superstars Fall Out Boy and Panic! at the Disco, MTV Video Music Award nominee and three-time Grammy winner Paramore stood out from the crowd with the addition of the band's bright-orange-haired front woman, Hayley Williams, whose relatable lyrics and infectious stage presence made her the definitive "Crushcrushcrush" of teens throughout the mid-2000s. After emerging with its 2005 debut studio album, *All We Know Is Falling*, which includes early favorites "Pressure" and "Emergency," Paramore took a giant leap to fame with its next record, 2007's *Riot!*, which features its biggest hit and major breakthrough, "Misery Business," a modern emo classic that became the band's first six-times-platinum song in 2022.

In 2013, the band enjoyed its first number one on the US *Billboard* 200 with its self-titled fourth studio album. But that success was somewhat overshadowed by the highly publicized 2010 exits of founding guitarist Josh Farro and his younger brother, founding drummer Zac Farro, whose departures left a sour taste in the mouths of fans who had been there since day one. By 2015, Williams was the only original member left, but the 2017 return of Zac Farro (plus the 2009 addition of former touring guitarist Taylor York) steadied the ship and has since resulted in the release of Paramore's most acclaimed works, 2017's *After Laughter* and 2023's *This Is Why*, earning the band a coveted spot opening for Taylor Swift on the culturally phenomenal 2023-2024 Eras Tour.

### 40. Puddle of Mudd

Although controversy seems to have followed Puddle of Mudd around over the last decade, mainly due to the onstage antics (including accusations of miming) and offstage problems (including numerous domestic violence and drunk and disorderly charges) of lead singer/rhythm guitarist and sole remaining original member Wes Scantlin, the early 2000s were kind to the post-grunge band, who benefited from the genre's second wave of mainstream popularity at the turn of the century. Kicking off with its three-times-platinum 2001 debut studio album, *Come Clean*, released through Fred Durst's Flawless Records, the band refined the songs and sound of its early demos to create one of the biggest debuts for any post-grunge artist, eventually pushing the record to number nine on the US *Billboard* 200 in early 2002.

The success of the album's second single, "Blurry," which peaked at number five on the US *Billboard* Hot 100 and hit number one on both the US *Billboard* Mainstream Rock and Modern Rock Tracks charts, also helped Puddle of Mudd top the latter chart with the band's subsequent three consecutive releases, an impressive feat by any measure. ("Blurry" would also secure Puddle of Mudd two wins at the 2002 *Billboard* Music Awards, a win for Best Single at the 2002 *Kerrang!* Awards, and a Best New Artist in a Video nomination at the 2002 MTV Video Music Awards.) The band has since sold over seven million records worldwide but has struggled to maintain the respect of many in the rock world due to Scantlin's legal issues, controversies, and the constant hiring and firing of members.

### 41. Queens of the Stone Age

After the demise of seminal Palm Desert stoner rock band Kyuss, few could've expected some of its members to go on to start one of the most successful and acclaimed rock bands of the twenty-first century. But that's precisely what happened when former Kyuss guitarist Josh Homme decided to form Queens of the Stone Age, a band that has so far accumulated nine Grammy nominations, in 1996. Now front and center and playing every instrument (bar drums) on the band's self-titled 1998 debut studio album, Homme—its only continual member throughout its history—injected Queens of the Stone Age with the desert rock grooves of Kyuss and the cock rock bluster of Mick Jagger and Roger Daltrey, creating one of the most distinctive bodies of work in modern alternative music.

While Queens of the Stone Age's debut record, and 2000's follow-up, *Rated R*, performed reasonably around the world, 2002's *Songs for the Deaf*—its first gold-certified studio album in the US—took the band to the next level, peaking at number seventeen on the US *Billboard* 200 and number four in the UK respectively. (With *Songs for the Deaf*'s second single, "Go with the Flow," the band took home one award—from three nominations—at the 2003 MTV Video Music Awards.) In 2013, Queens of the Stone Age's success would extend to its first number one on the US *Billboard* 200 with the release of its sixth studio album, *. . . Like Clockwork*, which sold over ninety-one thousand copies in its first week. The band's eighth and latest studio album, *In Times New Roman . . .*, was released in 2023.

## 42. Seether

Emerging from inside the hills of the Magaliesberg mountain range in Pretoria, South Africa, post-grunge's Seether initially found fame in its homeland under a different name, Saron Gas, but was told to change it once it had relocated to North America and signed with Wind-up Records. Spurred on by the release of its first single, "Fine Again," which peaked at number three on the US *Billboard* Mainstream Rock chart and remains one of its most well-known songs, the resulting debut studio album, 2002's *Disclaimer*, a mix of new songs and rerecorded tracks written while performing as Saron Gas, was an immediate success in North America, peaking at number ninety-two on the US *Billboard* 200 and earning the band a gold record on its first attempt.

The era-defining rock radio classic "Broken," which features vocals from Amy Lee of Evanescence fame, continued Seether's rise up the charts, peaking at number twenty on the US *Billboard* Hot 100 and becoming its first four-times-platinum-certified song. But success didn't stop there for the foursome, whose upward trajectory has shown no signs of slowing down. The band's highest peak of number two on the US *Billboard* 200 came with its 2011 fifth studio album, *Holding Onto Strings Better Left to Fray*, while the song "Wasteland" from its 2020 eighth studio album, *Si Vis Pacem, Para Bellum*, became its ninth chart-topper on the US *Billboard* Mainstream Rock chart. Seether's ninth and most recent studio album, *The Surface Seems So Far*, was released in 2024.

### 43. Simple Plan

Named after the lesser-known 1998 Sam Raimi-directed neonoir crime thriller film, Simple Plan released its debut studio album, *No Pads, No Helmets . . . Just Balls*, in 2002. The album, sounding like an adolescent love letter to bands like Blink-182 and Good Charlotte, features Mark Hoppus from the former and Joel Madden from the latter on backing vocals, signaling both bands' importance to the second wave of pop-punk. While some critics pushed back against the album's alleged lack of originality, the record was a hit among teens across North America, peaking at number thirty-five on the US *Billboard* 200 and earning two-times-platinum status in just under two years.

While the success of Simple Plan's debut record rewarded the band with a nomination for Best New Artist in a Video for the song "Addicted" at the 2003 MTV Video Music Awards and gave it the opportunity to open for artists like Blink-182, Green Day, and Avril Lavigne, the band's 2004 second studio album, *Still Not Getting Any . . .*, resulted in its biggest commercial hit to date, peaking at number three on the US *Billboard* 200 with opening week sales of over 139,000 copies. (The band achieved another VMA nomination—for Best Editing in a Video—in 2004.) Now six studio albums deep into its career, Simple Plan released its latest record, *Harder Than It Looks*, in 2022.

### 44. Slipknot

When your band consists of nine uniquely creative and chaotically individual members, it's almost inevitable that egos and musical differences will cause vitriol and tensions over several decades. But while the masked members of Slipknot have not only had to deal with a revolving door of musicians and the tragic deaths of two of the band's founders, bassist

Paul Gray in 2010 and drummer Joey Jordison in 2021, the band has continued in the face of adversity, going from strength to strength in the years since the 1999 release of its groundbreaking eponymous debut studio album. (In a 2020 retrospective, *Kerrang!* placed said album, *Slipknot*, atop its list of "The 50 Best Albums from 1999.")

And despite Slipknot's offstage conflicts being every bit as turbulent as its onstage live shows, the band has remained one of the driving forces in modern metal throughout its existence, winning one Grammy from eleven nominations and seven wins from twenty-four nominations at the *Kerrang!* Awards and has sold over thirty million albums worldwide. (In 2008, Slipknot also achieved its first of three consecutive number ones on the US *Billboard* 200 with the release of its fourth studio album, *All Hope Is Gone*, earning a first-time nomination at the MTV Video Music Awards for the album's first single, "Psychosocial.") Slipknot's seventh, latest, and final studio album under contract at Roadrunner Records, *The End, So Far*, was released in 2022.

### 45. Staind

Putting the unfortunate politics of front man Aaron Lewis aside, Staind emerged from the 1990s alternative scene with a style that not only blended the sounds of nu-metal and post-grunge but also actively avoided both genres' trappings by leaning into the lyrical themes of sadness and solidarity that made grunge so relatable at the start of the decade. Specifically echoing the heaviness of Alice in Chains's original lead vocalist Layne Staley's deeply personal lyrics, Staind introduced itself to the world with its self-released 1996 debut studio album, *Tormented*, which caught the attention of Limp Bizkit's Fred Durst, who signed the band to its first record deal with Flip Records the following year.

Staind's next record, 1999's *Dysfunction*, was the band's breakthrough, peaking at number seventy-four on the US *Billboard* 200 chart before eventually going two-times-platinum in 2004. However, that success only scratched the surface of what Staind would achieve in the following years. Each of its subsequent three studio albums—2001's *Break the Cycle*, 2003's *14 Shades of Grey*, and 2005's *Chapter V*—debuted atop the US *Billboard* 200, earning the band its first two of three chart-topping songs on the US *Billboard* Modern Rock Tracks chart and its first three of five number ones on the US *Billboard* Mainstream Rock chart. (Staind earned its only MTV VMA nomination—for Best Rock Video—in 2001.)

### 46. Sum 41

Though it initially presented itself as a pop-punk band with its platinum-selling Jerry Finn-produced 2001 debut studio album, *All Killer No Filler*, you'd be hard-pressed to find a more eclectic discography than that of Sum 41's. Shifting from pop-punk and heavy metal to melodic hardcore and alternative rock, the band has never allowed itself to be pigeonholed into any one category, continually pushing against the boundaries of any specific genre. That being said, Sum 41 will always be remembered for its pop-punk beginnings, and it's with that sound that the band found its greatest success with songs like "Fat Lip" and "In Too Deep," which peaked at number eight and thirteen in the UK respectively.

But despite Sum 41's achievements, including a nomination at the MTV Video Music Awards in 2001, a Grammy nomination in 2012, and three chart-topping hits on the US *Billboard* Modern Rock Tracks chart, the band announced on May 8, 2023, that it would be dissolving following the release of one final studio album and a farewell tour, bringing an end to one of the most popular bands of the MTV2 Generation. Sum 41's eighth and final studio album, *Heaven :x: Hell*, a double record celebrating its diverse sound, was released on March 29, 2024. Fittingly, the band's final two shows took place in front of its fellow Canadians at the Scotiabank Arena in Toronto on January 28 and 30, 2025.

### 47. System of a Down

From its self-titled 1998 debut studio album to its fifth and most recent record, 2005's *Hypnotize*, Armenian-American heavy metal band System of a Down, thanks to its Frank Zappa-like exploration of musical experimentation, has set itself apart from contemporaneous macho-posturing nu-metal bands, acting as the antithesis to the music that was dominating the charts at the end of the 1990s. With its distinct combination of avant-garde arrangements and thematically heavy lyrics, the band arguably became the most politically minded, critically acclaimed, and commercially successful rock group to bring themes like war, genocide, and social injustice to the masses since Rage Against the Machine burst onto the scene at the beginning of the decade.

Surprisingly, though, System of a Down's overtly political music hasn't seemed to hurt record sales, as the band has charted two songs atop the US *Billboard* Modern Rock Tracks chart and debuted three chart-topping albums on the US *Billboard* 200 and has sold over twelve million records worldwide. Awards recognition has followed the band throughout its existence too; System of a Down has been nominated for three MTV Video Music Awards and won one Grammy from four nominations, in addition to being named Best International Live Act at the 1999 *Kerrang!* Awards. In 2020, the band released its first new music in fifteen years, the double A-side single "Protect the Land/Genocidal Humanoidz," which raised over $600,000 in donations for the Armenia Fund in the wake of the Second Nagorno-Karabakh War.

## 48. Trivium

Any attempt to try and match the commercial heights of bands like Metallica and Megadeth would be a fool's errand. But Grammy-nominated Trivium stands as the heir apparent to the thrash metal titans, earning its place among the leaders of the new wave of American heavy metal movement that exploded during the early 2000s. Led by lead singer/guitarist Matt Heafy, who in 2006, at the tender age of twenty, became the youngest recipient of the *Metal Hammer* Golden God Award, the band has worked tirelessly since the 2003 release of its debut studio album, *Ember to Inferno*, releasing a further nine records (its tenth and latest being 2021's *In the Court of the Dragon*) and continuing to sell out shows worldwide year after year.

While *Ember to Inferno*, written and recorded when Heafy was just seventeen years old, gave Trivium a seat at the heavy metal table, its follow-up record, 2005's *Ascendancy*, immediately pushed the band to the top of the new wave of American heavy metal pack. (*Ascendancy*, acclaimed as 2005's "Album of the Year" by *Kerrang!* magazine, has since shipped over 100,000 copies in the UK alone and earned the band its first gold record.) In 2025, Trivium celebrated the twentieth anniversary of *Ascendancy* by embarking on a coheadline tour with fellow modern metal giant Bullet for My Valentine, which was celebrating the twentieth anniversary of its debut record, *The Poison*.

## 49. Weezer

Everyone's favorite nerdy rock band, Weezer, made being a geek cool long before a generation of kids jumped on the bandwagon of the Marvel Cinematic Universe and normalized liking comic books instead of harassing those who read them. Weezer initially set itself apart by refusing to buckle under the pressure of grunge and pretend to be something it's not, choosing instead to lean into its geeky tendencies with the release of its five-times-platinum 1994 debut, *The Blue Album*. It's during this time that the band also perfected the art of the music video and got substantial airplay on MTV. (Its Spike Jonze-directed video for the album's second and most successful single, "Buddy Holly," took home four awards from five nominations at the 1995 MTV Video Music Awards.)

Over thirty years into the band's career, Weezer has maintained relevancy through consistency, remaining as down to earth today as on the day it started. In 2005, the song "Beverly Hills," the band's first single from its hit fifth studio album, *Make Believe*, became its first of eight chart-toppers on the US *Billboard* Modern Rock Tracks chart, and in 2009, Weezer would win Best Music Video at the Grammy Awards—its first and only Grammy from five nominations—for "Pork and Beans." (The video for "Pork and Beans" also earned the band its fifth MTV Video Music Award, after topping the US *Billboard* Modern Rock Tracks chart the year before.) Weezer's fifteenth and most recent studio album, *Van Weezer*, was released in 2021.

## 50. Wheatus

"Teenage Dirtbag," the debut single from the band responsible for writing the song after which this book is named, was a worldwide hit for Wheatus, spending four weeks atop Australia's ARIA Singles Chart and ending 2000 as the country's second-best-selling single, behind only Anistasia's "I'm Outta Love." Despite the song's modest success in the band's homeland, peaking at number seven on the US *Billboard* Modern Rock Tracks chart, and partially inspired by the childhood of front man and sole remaining original member Brendan B. Brown, "Teenage

Dirtbag" became an outsider anthem for my generation's youth. A major success in the UK, the song spent two weeks at its peak position of number two in early 2001, missing out on the top spot only because of Atomic Kitten's first UK chart-topper, "Whole Again."

The "Teenage Dirtbag" music video was also a hit, becoming a staple for alternative rock channels across the globe, and earning a Best Video nomination at the 2001 *Kerrang!* Awards. Based on Amy Heckerling's 2000 American teen romantic comedy film, *Loser*, the video features the film's costars and fellow *American Pie* alumni, Jason Biggs and Mena Suvari, as the story's affably eponymous loser and his seemingly unattainable love interest. Wheatus again achieved chart success in the UK with its cover of Erasure's synth-pop classic "A Little Respect," surpassing the fourth-place peak of Erasure's 1988 original by one spot in mid-2001. (In 2025, "Teenage Dirtbag" placed at number 241 on *Rolling Stone*'s list of "The 250 Greatest Songs of the 21st Century So Far.")

*CHAPTER 12*
# Still Just a Teenage Dirtbag, Baby: A Conversation with Wheatus Founder Brendan B. Brown

Believe it or not, I had this book's title stuck in my head long before I started putting words to the page. Consequently, after outlining all the chapters within, I knew I wanted to end this examination of the MTV2 Generation by talking to someone whose songs soundtracked my childhood years. I would've been delighted to speak to anyone from the list above, but there's really only one person whose signature song, "Teenage Dirtbag," became the definitive teen anthem of my youth. Thus, as luck would have it, the music gods must've been listening to my wishes when Brendan B. Brown, the Wheatus star and songwriter behind "Teenage Dirtbag," agreed to join me for an hourlong conversation about his childhood dreams, his musical journey so far, and Wheatus's future plans.

It was truly a privilege to speak to a musician I've admired for twenty-five years, and I couldn't have wished for a better subject to close out this book.

So, without any further hesitation, please enjoy my conversation with the original teenage dirtbag himself, the one and only Brendan B. Brown.

**Jon Sheasby:** Hi, Brendan. I know how busy you are with touring, so I'm enormously grateful you were able to find some time in your day to speak to me.

**Brendan B. Brown:** No, no worries. Thanks for covering us as part of your book.

**Jon Sheasby:** Of course! So, when you started Wheatus in 1995, what were your ambitions for the band and yourself in general? Was being a full-time musician always the dream?

**Brendan B. Brown:** Definitely. Since I was ten years old, I wanted to be some sort of professional musician. Of course, when you're ten, you've got big dreams and little ideas. I came through college as a guitarist, auditioning in bands in New York and just trying to find my place. And I think that when I started Wheatus, the goal was to see if I could be the front person, the singer-songwriter, of a band. I was trying to find my voice and what kind of guitar player I wanted to be. So I spent a lot of time in the woodshed, in the laboratory, with a four-track and a drum machine, just making sure it didn't sound stupid. [Laughs.] I think, at that point, that was the idea. At least that was the goal—to see if I could front a band myself.

**Jon Sheasby:** Who were your primary influences when you were starting out?

**Brendan B. Brown:** I have a lot of influences going all the way back to Willie Nelson, the Temptations, Prince, AC/DC, Rush, Metallica, Cyndi Lauper, Run D.M.C., LL Cool J, Public Enemy, Paul Simon. When I started to do the singing and songwriting for my own band, I was really beginning to get deeply into Tom Petty and the Heartbreakers, Ani DiFranco, Fugazi, and the Pixies. I was also paying a lot of attention to how the Indigo Girls' *Rites of Passage* [the band's 1992 fourth studio album] sounded and how it was produced. Then, on the more contemporary side, there's Foo Fighters, Smashing Pumpkins, and Dinosaur Jr., who were an early influence on my guitar sound. Also, I had been in a band called Hope Factory, and the singer-songwriter was another guy I was taking direction from. He had been really into bands like Curve, Echobelly, Blur, My Bloody Valentine, and all those British bands. Before that, I had only really heard of Erasure, Depeche Mode, the Smiths, and the more popular stuff that predated Oasis. So I would say it was a good mix of childhood influences and stuff that was modern and inspiring at the same time.

**Jon Sheasby:** How was gigging with Wheatus when the band first started? Did you play primarily covers or start writing/performing original songs from the get-go?

**Brendan B. Brown:** Mostly originals from the get-go. We were very cautious about it because I had learned a few times in a row in different bands that New York City is a place where you can wear your crowd out in one or two shows. We were very careful and played only once every two or three months. We made sure that we had some good covers in the set, but we never led with them. We had an eclectic mix of covers like "Mammas Don't Let Your Babies Grow Up to Be Cowboys" and Cheap Trick's "Surrender." Stuff like "Jesse's Girl" by Rick Springfield and "Beat on the Brat" by the Ramones. We just mixed it up the best we could, and Erasure's "A Little Respect" was one of those early covers.

**Jon Sheasby:** The band was formed on the Lower East Side of New York City, and in 1999, you booked a regular spot at the Luna Lounge, a venue famed for its mixture of music and stand-up comedy, which regularly featured the likes of Sarah Silverman, Marc Maron, Patton Oswalt, the Strokes, Interpol, and yourselves, to name but a few. From the outside, it appears the New York art scene was thriving in the late 1990s/early 2000s, but how did it feel from the inside? Was there a palpable sense of excitement in the air for all these emerging talents?

**Brendan B. Brown:** We primarily bounced back and forth between two clubs. We played the Luna Lounge on Ludlow Street, and right around the corner we played the Mercury Lounge on East Houston Street. But [Luna Lounge owner] Robert Sacher was a real music guy. He was very practical, kind, and soft-spoken, which was different for New York. [Laughs.] He was laid-back, but he wasn't there for your bullshit. He genuinely cared about—and was a fan of—the music, the comedy, and whatever else he gave his space to. So I would say Rob was unique in the entire experience in the New York City music scene. He was like no other, really, and was extremely generous and tolerant because sometimes the crowds would get a little drunk, and you brought these people to his establishment. But he really helped start something, and his generosity gave an exponential degree of energy to the scene that normally wouldn't have been there. He didn't charge people to come in and wasn't trying to make money off the artists. He was just trying to see if their friends would buy his beer. [Laughs.] He kept it on a lower, more independent commerce level that was a bit more realistic and easier to deal with, whereas other clubs were a money deal from the start.

**Jon Sheasby:** How did it feel, then, to eventually sign with a major label, Columbia Records, and see your self-titled debut [released on August 15, 2000] chart all over the world?

**Brendan B. Brown:** That's an interesting question. We didn't chart all over the world initially. For the first five or six months or so, nothing really happened. In fact, when we first blew up in Australia, that was at a point during which the record label had stopped calling us back. I think they had begun to move on from whatever that first record of ours was meant to do, and then Australia picked it up and did something with it. Then the UK followed suit and most of the territories in Europe, and eventually it came all the way back around to America.

**Jon Sheasby:** And, of course, it'd be remiss of me not to talk about your biggest hit and the song after which this book is named, "Teenage Dirtbag," which continues to connect with the kids of today in the same way it did with my generation back in 2000.

**Brendan B. Brown:** Yeah, that all happened when One Direction started to cover the song. And then, about seven or eight years after that, it blew up on TikTok, and for the first time ever, the US sales and streams exceeded that of what goes on overseas. So it took twenty years before it finally came back around in the US, but it was accepted overseas in Australia and the UK first. It was a long time coming, and for me and the band, the practical reality is that we never got used to being a big act. We never got used to being famous. A little bit overseas, but certainly not in the US when we came home to live in our mom's house. [Laughs.] It doesn't feel like you've accomplished much.

**Jon Sheasby:** [Laughs.] What's it like from this vantage point, knowing you're responsible for writing one of the definitive teenage anthems of all time?

**Brendan B. Brown:** Well, I've always been looking out for it to end. [Laughs.] Most of our survival as a band has been through incredible scarcity and not anything that's felt anywhere near stable or sustainable. We just learned how to approach the whole thing that way over many, many years. It was not until the end of our second decade that we remotely began to feel like things were stabilizing. So we didn't get used to it. And when you say something like that, a part of me knows that's a reality, and that's how "Teenage Dirtbag" is perceived. But in my daily life, I have never been able to practice any sort of absorption of that into my worldview because I've spent so much time not feeling that way about it. That being said, I love the song and still love playing it live, and it's always been enjoyable that way.

Whether it was 2008/2009, when there was really nothing going on, or when Quincy Jones did a version of it on TikTok, throughout those two extremes, we've always appreciated the song, and that's never faded. So we kind of still see it in that way—the way we saw it when we enjoyed playing it during the darkest times. But it's very difficult to verbalize it being an anthem and all that stuff. As you can tell, I'm struggling to put words together to tell you how I feel about it because most of our time was spent trying to survive. Maybe one day we'll get a big multimillion-dollar check for it. [Laughs.] Until then, we'll keep trying to keep it lean and nimble because that's how we learn to survive.

**Jon Sheasby:** I'd also love to know how the connection between the iconic "Teenage Dirtbag" music video and Amy Heckerling's 2000 film, *Loser*, came about. Was that something that was pitched to you, or was it just a happy coincidence?

**Brendan B. Brown:** It was both a coincidence and it was pitched to us. We were signed to Columbia Records, and Amy was putting *Loser* out through Columbia TriStar, both of which were under the Sony umbrella. And I think somebody at the Sony film department said, "Oh, look at this nice piece of music here. Maybe we could stick it in the movie." And that somebody, I found out later, was her. [Laughs.] Amy wanted the song in her film, and of course she's a really musically oriented filmmaker. Some of the most iconic music moments in cinema are from her, so we jumped at it when we found out she was interested and decided to trust that she knew what she was talking about. I'm quite happy that we did because we accomplished two goals that—for me personally—I never imagined would happen. First, we had a song in a film while Elwood Blues [Dan Aykroyd's character from *The Blues Brothers*] was onscreen.

As a fan of *The Blues Brothers*, I was floored because that is the most important musical movie of my entire life. For me, more than *Grease* or *Back to the Future* or any of those touchstones, *The Blues Brothers* is the ultimate music movie. I knew who Ray Charles was, but I never *really* knew until I watched *The Blues Brothers* and began to understand Aretha Franklin, James Brown, and the rest. You know, we wound up opening for James Brown in Belgium. That was just so profound, and that's one thing about *Loser* that really made me happy. And then the second, being a New York band, is that "Teenage Dirtbag" played during a helicopter shot of the World Trade Center, our skyline, our hometown skyline. Those are two things that just couldn't be beaten, and it was a really incredible opportunity and dream come true for us to have Amy use our song in those two ways. It blew us out of the water. It was crazy.

**Jon Sheasby:** How difficult was it, then, to leave Columbia after the release of your 2003 second studio album, *Hand Over Your Loved Ones*, and start afresh, creating your own label, Montauk Mantis, through which you continue to release new music? Did it feel like a defeat at the time, and in hindsight, does that freedom—independent of a major label—give you a space to be more creatively expressive?

**Brendan B. Brown:** At the time, it felt like we were entering a wilderness, and there were no real independent distribution systems for music yet. iTunes and the iPod were barely beginning to show any sort of significance. YouTube wasn't there yet. And forget all the other distribution systems for independent music because none existed. So we didn't know what we were diving into. Honestly, it was a bit of a relief to be off the label at the time because they were flatly refusing to release our second record, which we found really confusing considering we recouped on our first. We were kind of baffled by that. We left, got our masters for the second album back, and immediately started to figure out how to release it. "What do we do, and what do we spend our money on? Do you sign a distribution deal? What platform is there for this? What exists?" Honestly, it didn't seem like there was much interest in anything we had done. Nobody was interested in what else we had to say at that point.

So we just battened down the hatches and became the best independent touring band that we could afford to be. Selling the record ourselves on tour was a thing, and poking around independent distribution deals was a thing, but none of it materialized. None of it came to anything. I think Twitter and TuneCore coming along around the same time changed the game, and you could begin to build a steady presence with independent touring and distribution. But between 2003 and 2009, those six years were very dark and difficult. We slowly crawled out of it, starting around 2010, and then, by 2016, we were on tour with Busted, doing an arena tour, and our publishing company finally noticed that they accidentally dropped us in 2007. So, they resigned us. [Laughs.] It was almost like we got lost in the shuffle of the changing industry. And at the time, although it looked very dismal, it actually turned out to be for the better because we emerged from that with no terrible management contract or record deal. We were free agents with a hit, which turned out to be much better for us in the long run. But I couldn't have said anything like that in 2007/2008. I would have thought quite the opposite. I would have told you, "Well, this is probably our last tour."

**Jon Sheasby:** I'd love to chat with you about touring, which seems to be a love/hate endeavor for most musicians. Having seemingly toured around the world endlessly for the best part of twenty-five years, what are some of your favorite memories from being on the road?

**Brendan B. Brown:** I love being on the road! The way that we do it is that we prepare for as long as we can. We try to stay healthy, sleep well, and take care of each other. Favorite memories from being on the road? Oh man, we love going out with Bowling for Soup. We toured with them in 2007, sold out that tour in the UK, and we just toured with them again in 2024 in the US, which was nearly sold out. My memories of touring with them are really fond, and it's sort of like we finally found a touring partner. It's really quite lovely. I could sit here and tell you the strangest stories. Great ones. Sad ones. Dangerous ones. I was caught in the crossfire of a gunfight in Canada once.

**Jon Sheasby:** [Laughs.] How was that?!

**Brendan B. Brown:** It was a quiet Sunday morning; the bus was parked in the back of a club, and I went out to change my laundry and put on a new pair of pants, and gunfire erupted while I was changing. [Laughs.] I was out in the open, so I had to dive into the bottom of the bus and close the door, and a couple of guys were trying to kill each other. It was in Canada, and I grew up in New York, so I said to myself, "There's no way I'm dying up here." [Laughs.] And then, like I said, we opened up for James Brown in Belgium. We opened for Paramore in New Jersey a few years ago. We were out with Jimmy Eat World just a few weeks ago. Basically, I'm saying that profound memories happen when you're both a fan and a performer in equal measure. It's an overwhelming combination of stimuli, as somebody who performs and listens to music. Those are the ones that stick with me. Also, the only time we ever played at CBGB was opening for Joey Ramone and Ronnie Spector in August 2000.

**Jon Sheasby:** Oh, how awesome!

**Brendan B. Brown:** It was fantastic. It was everything you would imagine it was. I had seen many shows there, but this was a different thing. This was, "Wow, we're really here with them. How did we fool them into letting us do this?" [Laughs.] There are too many fond memories to count, most of which are profoundly emotional musical experiences getting to see or work with people you've looked up to for many years.

**Jon Sheasby:** And I know you love returning over here quite often, and some of the band's biggest chart success has been achieved on these shores. So does the UK feel like a second home to you?

**Brendan B. Brown:** Always has. In fact, it's always felt like our first home, and the reason is that it was the first place in the world we were able to tour sustainably and return to tour again and again. We fit in there like a glove at this point. I love an English breakfast. I love a Sunday roast. We actually lived in Angel, London, for about eighteen months. So, it's always been a second-first home, not a second home but a second-first home.

**Jon Sheasby:** That's nice to hear. One of the opinions I hold about the music industry is that no one member is bigger than the band, and being in a musical collective is like any other working environment. People come and go, but that doesn't stop the band from being the band. It's the music that's most important, and still having the opportunity to see it performed live is paramount to anything else. Given that you're the sole remaining original member of your band, was there ever a time when you thought about calling it a day, or has Wheatus's existence never been in doubt?

**Brendan B. Brown:** I've never really understood what else I would do with my life. I thought about becoming a welder here and there when it got really hard. [Laughs.] But I started the band alone, right? I spent the first three years without a band. It was just myself with a four-track, a drum machine, and a bass. And for a long time, I've also understood the practical reality that other musicians will have different opportunities, and it's wrong to try and hold them back from those things. So, if Matthew [Milligan] were to find something important to him that he needed to do, I would want him to go and do it. I wouldn't want him

Recording Wheatus's self-titled debut studio album
Courtesy of Vicky Markey/Matthew Milligan

to sidetrack it so that he could continue out of some sense of loyalty. I don't feel like that's a good way to treat people you work with, to demand that they stay. If your project is good enough, they will stay; if it's not, they'll leave. And I've always approached it that way because, like I said, Wheatus was a solitary endeavor at its inception, so who am I to ask anybody to stick around? I'm still very good friends with [Phillip A. Jiminez] and [Mike Joseph McCabe], and my brother [Peter McCarrick Brown] was the first drummer for the band. And the extended family of many, many members of this band are still in communication with me. We're still friends, and I think that's more valuable than whatever weird sense of loyalty some people would superimpose onto these very complex relationships.

**Jon Sheasby:** I think that's a very mature way of handling things.

**Brendan B. Brown:** I've been lucky to work with people interested enough in Wheatus to help me do what I'm trying to do, so I don't have any complaints in that regard. I know the music that we display now is not music that the first version of the band could have done. We weren't capable of it, and it required different people, influences, spells, techniques, and disciplines. I think it's something like ninety percent of the drummers we've had have had a Latin percussion background, and that seems to be the formula that helps me compose with people on the drums. And the keyboard players have more often than not had some sort of classical training. Shannon Harris, our keyboard player on albums two and three, is now playing with Jeff Lynne's ELO. So we've had to look for relationships based on the requirements of what I'm trying to say with the songs. That casts a broader net by default and becomes an ongoing creative experiment, not a stodgy exercise in some concept of loyalty. I'm not interested in that. I'm really not interested in that kind of relationship. I'd much rather have a free-flowing circus of ideas.

**Jon Sheasby:** In late 2023, you released a fully rerecorded and reimagined version of your debut album, *Wheatus 2020*, now expanded to twenty tracks, with ten newly recorded songs unearthed from the band's vault. How did the genesis of that project come about, and what was it like to revisit and reimagine those songs over twenty years later?

**Brendan B. Brown:** So, that was years in the making. I don't know if you know about this, but it seems to be the case that the original masters are lost.

**Jon Sheasby:** I have read that, yeah.

**Brendan B. Brown:** And even *Rolling Stone* reached out to the label and asked them to confirm or deny their existence. And they were ghosted. So we have to assume the answer is not the one we're looking for. I began to suspect this was the case around 2012/2013 because we had quite a few licenses come in for sync requests that required the original multitrack.

And I approved them. I approved them all. And one by one, they died on the vine. I began to suspect that there was no master to complete the agreement because why else would they all die like that? Consequently, I started preparing to maybe rerecord our first album, thinking it was lost. In 2013/2014, I took the penultimate set of master tapes that I had, which was actually incomplete, and transferred them over to Pro Tools for the first time. We were then able to digitally assemble about seventy-five percent of the original album's multitrack. What was missing was some guitar solos, some vocals, and a lot of percussion. Basically, the last week of recording wasn't there. But from that, we were able to acquire all of the click tracks, drums, bass, primary guitars, and some vocals, and the net result was that we were able to replace one instrument at a time and rerecord the album as faithfully as we could.

We did that in bits and pieces, and it took us from 2015 until we finished the entirety of that album—twenty songs like you said—in 2023. We finished "Teenage Dirtbag" in 2020 because we wanted to finish that one for the twentieth anniversary of the song. Of course, the pandemic happened right then and there. And when COVID happened, it kind of stopped us from being able to finish the rest of what we'd been working on. It was 2023 when we finally got our act together and ended the process. And now it's out, and we have it on vinyl for the first time too. So it's the original album excluding the two songs I didn't write, which were replaced by two B-sides, plus ten demos that we studied and pieced together and rerecorded, and they sound like they could've belonged on our first record. We got those out of the vault, called them the "Lost Songs" series, and got a double LP out of it. We figured it's been twenty years since the original album, so why don't we put out twenty songs to reflect that? Because more is better, right? [Laughs.]

**Jon Sheasby:** Always. [Laughs.]

**Brendan B. Brown:** So we really enjoyed the process. It was challenging but very rewarding at the end. It was cool to look back at our immature first swipe at it all and do it again. It was fun.

**Jon Sheasby:** I'd also love to get your thoughts on Download Festival

2024, which I believe was your first appearance at Donington Park, right?

**Brendan B. Brown:** Yeah, our very first time. We were honored to be part of it. We couldn't believe that we got invited because, growing up, that was always the real metal festival, you know? But it was awesome to be there. I was a little ill, if I'm being totally honest. I wasn't at my best. But the crowd really made me feel like it wasn't a problem. We just really enjoyed ourselves and had a great show in the mud. Then, later on, I was invited to play an acoustic set in another tent, and I must say that that was the more interesting part of the evening when, for whatever reason, my voice cleared up a little. I was feeling strong again after being ill all day, and I was able to connect in a way with that UK audience that I had never connected with any UK audience in the past. It was just me, my guitar, and our backing vocalists, and it was just killer. It was so good.

*Wheatus* by Wheatus
Courtesy of Columbia Records

**Jon Sheasby:** There's always something special about festival crowds.

**Brendan B. Brown:** The crowd there was really spectacular.

**Jon Sheasby:** The first time I saw Black Sabbath, my favorite band of all time, was at Download Festival in 2012. And Soundgarden were on right before as well, and that was the only time I ever got to see Chris Cornell before he passed away. So that festival will always remain special to me.

**Brendan B. Brown:** Oh wow. It's funny you should mention that because in 2014, we played with both bands in London at another festival in Hyde Park. I have always been a huge Soundgarden fan, but I have to be honest and say that Sabbath was never really one of my top favorites. I love them, but they're not one of my tops. That day, though, Sabbath blew me out of water. I couldn't believe how good they were. Soundgarden opened for them; that was the third time I'd seen Soundgarden. So to play with Soundgarden and Sabbath on the same bill was really rewarding. One of those things you asked me before about touring—that was one of those "I can't believe this is happening" moments.

**Jon Sheasby:** And it appeared to me that the 2024 edition of Download was the unofficial pop-punk nostalgia year, given the inclusion of yourselves, the Offspring, Fall Out Boy, Sum 41, Bowling for Soup, Busted, and many more. So, how was it for you being on the same lineup as so many of your contemporaries and friends?

**Brendan B. Brown:** It was fantastic. We're friends with the guys in Hoobastank, right?

**Jon Sheasby:** Right.

**Brendan B. Brown:** And we were hanging out with the Bowling for Soup guys, and then the Hoobastank guys came through, and they're like, "Oh, we're playing in an hour!" And I said, "Fantastic! I'll come and meet you guys and take some video footage." It turns out they were playing on a stage that was a little bit far away, and I missed the transport to get there. So I had to get my wellies on and run through the mud. And I'll never forget this. I had this moment where, as I'm walking towards the other stage, Limp Bizkit is on the stage behind me, and they're playing "Break Stuff" while I'm rambling through this mud that's nearly up to my knees.

**Jon Sheasby:** Just chaos, I imagine?

**Brendan B. Brown:** It was so funny. It was just one of those moments I wish people could've seen how nuts it was. Absolutely brilliant.

**Jon Sheasby:** Did you get to hang out with any of your friends while you were there?

**Brendan B. Brown:** Oh yeah, very much so. I hung out with James [Bourne] from Busted. Like I said, the Bowling for Soup guys. We also caught up with Zebrahead, who we hadn't seen in twenty-five years. I had a little bit of a hang with the Biohazard guys, whom I was a little too afraid to introduce myself to. [Laughs.] As I said, Hoobastank, our old friends. We bumped into a lot of people that day. I'm a huge fan of John Otto, the drummer for Limp Bizkit. I think he's one of the best drummers who's ever lived.

**Jon Sheasby:** I think the musicianship between that band's members is wildly underrated.

**Brendan B. Brown:** Yeah, they're a really incredible band. I was at the side of the stage while he was warming up on his kit, and I instantly fanned out to the max. Like, "Wow, this is great!" He's one of those guys who's a real player, a real genuine one-off classic player on his instrument. I think he's one of the best drummers out there.

**Jon Sheasby:** I don't think anyone in that band gets the credit for being as good as they are. They're all highly talented.

**Brendan B. Brown:** I think that's definitely true of that band. They're fantastic musicians, and their sound is completely unique. Don't get me started on Wes [Borland]. I could talk about him forever. I also met the guys from 311 for the first time at that festival, and that was one of those things you never think you'll get to do until you're doing it.

**Jon Sheasby:** I know it has been a while since your last studio album, 2013's *The Valentine LP*, so do you have any updates on future plans?

**Brendan B. Brown:** I think we'll have difficulty getting back into the studio to finish our next album before 2026. I am going to record an acoustic album as quickly as I can, but at some point, in 2026, we will finish that seventh album. In the meantime, we've got lots of touring to do. We're finally selling our first record ourselves, which is new for us, and there's a documentary being made about us called *You Might*

*Die*. A couple of guys followed us around during the darkest years and caught a lot of—if I'm being honest—me not being the best bandleader. [Laughs.] So at some point, we will have to show our friends what things were really like. But more on that later. We'll see when that gets finished.

**Jon Sheasby:** Alright then, Brendan. It was a real honor to chat with you today. Little did I think all those years ago that I'd be speaking to you for my book after hearing "Teenage Dirtbag" for the first time.

**Brendan B. Brown:** Thanks, man. This was really enjoyable. I appreciate you reaching out. I hope to meet you someday on tour out there in the world. I don't know where you live, but if you want to swing through one of these tour dates, let me know!

**Jon Sheasby:** I'm in Birmingham.

**Brendan B. Brown:** Oh, a Brummie, eh?

**Jon Sheasby:** That's right, yeah. [Laughs.]

**Brendan B. Brown:** So if you feel like coming through, let us know, e-mail us, and we'll get you on the list. We'll shake hands and maybe have a snack or something.

**Jon Sheasby:** I'd love that. That'd be amazing!

**Brendan B. Brown:** Alright, Jon. Well, thank you again.

**Jon Sheasby:** It was my pleasure. Cheers, Brendan.

# Bibliography

Alderslade, Merlin, Rich Hobson, Paul Travers, Dave Everley, Adam Brennan, Catherine Morris, Alec Chillingworth, et al. 2023. "The 50 Best Metal Albums of the 2000s." *Metal Hammer. Louder*. July 28, 2023. www.loudersound.com/features/the-50-best-metal-albums-of-the-2000s.

Baker, Soren. 1999. "Record Rack." *Los Angeles Times*. February 21, 1999. www.latimes.com/archives/la-xpm-1999-feb-21-ca-10040-story.html.

Banger Films. 2020. "Dee Snider Speaks out against Censorship at PMRC Hearing." YouTube. September 21, 2020. www.youtube.com/watch?v=d7XEufg_itU.

Chacksfield, Marc. 2023. "The Best Movie and TV Dads of All Time." *Shortlist*. June 18, 2023. www.shortlist.com/news/best-tv-film-dads-star-wars-simpsons-homer.

Davies, Claire. 2016. "Blink-182 Producer John Feldmann on the Band's Triumphant Return and the Music That Inspired Him." *MusicRadar*. July 21, 2016. www.musicradar.com/news/guitars/blink-182-producer-john-feldmann-on-the\bands-triumphant-return-and-the-music-that-inspired-him-640478.

Diehl, Matt. 1996. "Bush: Razorblade Suitcase: Music Reviews." *Rolling Stone*. November 13, 1996. www.rollingstone.com/artists/bush/albums/album/242869/review/5944129/razorblade_suitcase.

Ebert, Roger. 2002. "8 Mile Movie Review & Film Summary (2002)." www.rogerebert.com. November 8, 2002. www.rogerebert.com/reviews/8-mile-2002.

Gleiberman, Owen. 1999. "American Pie." *Entertainment Weekly*. July 9, 1999. www.ew.com/article/1999/07/09/american-pie-2/.

Jenkins, Mark. 1999. "Creed's True Calling." *The Washington Post*. September 28, 1999. www.washingtonpost.com/wp-srv/WPcap/1999-09/28/010r-092899-idx.html.

Kerrang! 2017. "The 51 Greatest Pop-Punk Albums of All Time." *Kerrang!* September 23, 2017. www.kerrang.com/the-51-greatest-pop-punk-albums-green-day-wonder-years-blink-2017.

Kerrang! 2021. "The 25 Greatest Emo Albums Ever." *Kerrang!* March 18, 2021. www.kerrang.com/the-25-greatest-emo-albums-ever.

Kreps, Daniel. 2014. "19 Worst Things about Woodstock '99." *Rolling Stone*. July 31, 2014. www.rollingstone.com/music/music-news/19-worst-things-about-woodstock-99-176052/.

Law, Sam. 2020. "The 21 Greatest Nu-Metal Albums of All Time." *Kerrang!* June 17, 2020. www.kerrang.com/the-21-greatest-nu-metal-albums-of-all-time-definitively-ranked.

Law, Sam. 2020. "The 50 Best Albums from 1999." *Kerrang!* July 10, 2020. www.kerrang.com/the-50-best-albums-from-1999.

Law, Sam. 2021. "'Being Thought of as a Joke Band Is Better than an "Art Band"': The Inside Story of Blink-182's Enema of the State." *Kerrang!* June 1, 2021. www.kerrang.com/blink-182-the-inside-story-of-enema-of-the-state.

Lipshutz, Jason. 2021. "Limp Bizkit Lollapalooza Recap: How Fred Durst & Co. Won." *Billboard*. August 1, 2021. www.billboard.com/culture/events/limp-bizkit-lollapalooza-recap-fred-durst-best-moments-9608812/.

Loudwire. 2016. "Disturbed's 'Down with the Sickness' Wins March Metal Madness 2016." *Loudwire*. April 5, 2016. www.loudwire.com/disturbed-down-with-the-sickness-wins-march-metal-madness-2016/.

Manson, Marilyn. 1999. "Columbine: Whose Fault Is It?" *Rolling Stone*. June 24, 1999. www.rollingstone.com/culture/culture-news/columbine-whose-fault-is-it-232759/.

Marchese, David. 2022. "Eddie Vedder Is Still Learning to Live with Loss." *The New York Times*. January 31, 2022. www.nytimes.com/interactive/2022/01/31/magazine/eddie-vedder-interview.html.

Masuo, Sandy. 1999. "Limp Bizkit Adds Some Depth to Its Hard-Hitting Attitude." *Los Angeles Times*. June 18, 1999. www.latimes.com/archives/la-xpm-1999-jun-18-ca-47631-story.html.

McMahon, James. 2019. "Korn's Jonathan Davis: 'I Have the Remains of at Least Seven People in My House.'" *NME*. September 13, 2019. www.nme.com/features/music-interviews/jonathan-davis-korn-interview-the-nothing-album-2019-human-remains-2547828.

Murphy, J Kim. 2024. "Marilyn Manson to Pay $327K to Evan Rachel Wood after Dropping Lawsuit." *Variety*. November 26, 2024. www.variety.com/2024/music/news/marilyn-manson-drops-lawsuit-evan-rachel-wood-legal-fees-1236224025/.

Newman, Jason. 2015. "Rage against the Machine Bassist: 'I Apologize for Limp Bizkit.'" *Rolling Stone*. September 29, 2015. www.rollingstone.com/music/musicfeatures/-32182/#ixzz3n9BPurRj.

Nolan, Christopher. 2008. *The Dark Knight*. United States: Warner Bros.

Ozzi, Dan. 2013. "Can Pop Punk Age Gracefully?" *Vice*. May 31, 2013. www.vice.com/en/article/can-pop-punk-age-gracefully/.

Radio X. 2022. "Here's What Fred Durst Said about Limp Bizkit's Woodstock '99 Performance." *Radio X*. August 9, 2022. www.radiox.co.uk/features/what-fred-durst-said-about-limp-bizkit-woodstock99/.

Rolling Stone. 2013. "Readers' Poll: The Ten Worst Bands of the Nineties." *Rolling Stone*. May 9, 2013. www.rollingstone.com/music/music-lists/readers-poll-the-ten-worst-bands-of-the-nineties-13654/.

Rolling Stone. 2025. "The 250 Greatest Songs of the 21st Century so Far." *Rolling Stone*. October 8, 2025. www.rollingstone.com/music/music-lists/best-songs-of-the-21st-century-1235410452/.

Siegel, Adam. 2019. "Comedy in the '90s, Part 4: 'American Pie,' the Raunchy Culmination of a Decade of Family-Friendly Films." *The Ringer*. September 24, 2019. www.theringer.com/2019/09/24/movies/american-pie-90s-comedy-home-alone.

Slate, Jeff. 2022. "Bob Dylan on Music's Golden Era vs. Streaming: 'Everything's Too Easy.'" *The Wall Street Journal*. December 19, 2022. www.wsj.com/articles/bob-dylan-interview-11671471665.

Slessor, Dan. 2020. "The 13 Most Essential Sludge Records." *Kerrang!* June 16, 2020. www.kerrang.com/13-essential-sludge-records.

Taylor, Magdalene. 2023. "Hear Me Out: Creed Are Finally Cool." *Vice*. November 17, 2023. www.vice.com/en/article/creed-band-music-cool-again/.

Wartofsky, Alona. 1999. "Woodstock's Bitter Ending." *The Washington Post*. July 29, 1999. www.washingtonpost.com/archive/lifestyle/1999/07/29/woodstocks-bitter-ending/e09943c8-0de2-4860-8249-80d4091fd49d/.

Weingarten, Christopher R. 2014. "Korn's 1994 Debut LP: The Oral History." *Rolling Stone*. December 11, 2014. www.rollingstone.com/music/music-news/korns-1994-debut-lp-the-oral-history-44821/.

Weingarten, Marc. 1999. "Record Rack." *Los Angeles Times*. September 25, 1999. www.latimes.com/archives/la-xpm-1999-sep-25-ca-14092-story.html.

Yarrow, Allison. 2018. *90s Bitch: Media, Culture, and the Failed Promise of Gender Equality*. New York: Harper Perennial.

# Acknowledgments

To my publishers, David Bushman and Scott Ryan: I can't thank you both enough for taking a chance on me and helping turn this book into something more than I could ever have imagined. Thank you for pushing me to make every chapter better and for your guidance throughout.

To P. R. Brown, Lauren Mayhew, Joel McIver, and Brendan B. Brown: Thank you for answering my e-mails, taking my calls, and being so charitable with your time. This book wouldn't have been possible without your contributions, and I'm eternally grateful to you all.

To Matthew Milligan and Cameron Moore: Thank you for all your help in setting up the interview with Brendan and for gifting me four tickets to see Wheatus (plus Bowling for Soup and Magnolia Park) at The Halls, Wolverhampton, on February 9, 2025. The entire Wheatus team's generosity has been beyond my wildest expectations, and I loved every second of the show. You guys rock!

To my parents, sister, and brother-in-law: Thank you for your endless support and encouragement. Especially from you two, Mom and Dad. I honestly couldn't have wished for better parents, and I love you both unconditionally.

And finally, to my little nephew: You're the light of our lives. I hope, when you're old enough to read this one day, it'll inspire you to chase your dreams.

Wheatus at The Halls, Wolverhampton, on February 9, 2025
Courtesy of the author

# ABOUT THE AUTHOR

Jon Sheasby is a UK based writer, musician, and film studies graduate from the University of Wolverhampton. He proudly hails from Birmingham, England, the same culturally diverse city that produced legendary heavy metal founder Black Sabbath, iconic reggae ensemble UB40, and celebrated new wave act Duran Duran. He first started writing online in 2017, primarily focusing on film, music, TV, and wrestling history. He staunchly defends the collecting of physical media and firmly opposes the use of AI in the creation of art. When not working on his latest project, Jon can be found supporting his beloved Aston Villa Football Club and dreaming of the club's first major trophy in three decades.

# MORE TO READ AT TUCKERDSPRESS.COM

# MORE TO READ AT TUCKERDSPRESS.COM

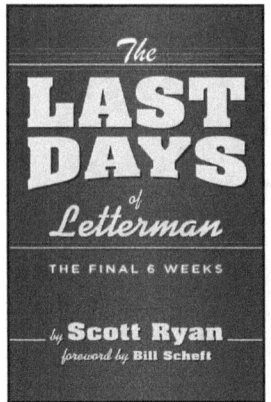

www.ingramcontent.com/pod-product-compliance
Lightning Source LLC
LaVergne TN
LVHW012107070526
838202LV00056B/5649